THE STAR SYSTEM

HOLLYWOOD'S PRODUCTION OF POPULAR IDENTITIES

PAUL MCDONALD

WALLFLOWER

LONDON

A Wallflower Paperback

First published in Great Britain in 2000 by
Wallflower Publishing Limited
16 Chalk Farm Road, Camden Lock, London NW1 8AG
www.wallflowerpress.co.uk

All stills courtesy of BFI Films: Stills, Posters and Designs
Used by permission

A catalogue record for this book is available from the British Library

ISBN 1 903364 02 7

Book Design by Rob Bowden Design

Typeset by LaserScript Ltd, Mitcham, Surrey

Printed in Great Britain by
Antony Rowe Ltd, Chippenham, Wiltshire

SHORT CUTS

INTRODUCTIONS TO FILM STUDIES

OTHER TITLES IN THE SHORT CUTS SERIES

THE HORROR GENRE: FROM BEELZEBUB TO BLAIR WITCH
Paul Wells

SCIENCE FICTION CINEMA: FROM OUTERSPACE TO CYBERSPACE
Geoff King and Tanya Krzywinska

EARLY SOVIET CINEMA: INNOVATION, IDEOLOGY AND PROPAGANDA
David Gillespie

CONTENTS

list of illustrations

tables and charts

acknowledgements

introduction: looking at stars 1

1   stardom as a system 5

2   making the system 15

3   controlling the system 40

4   rethinking the system 71

conclusion: stars and hollywood history 111

filmography

bibliography

index of names

LIST OF ILLUSTRATIONS

1   Mary Pickford **36**

2   Judy Garland **51**

3   James Cagney and Joan Leslie **67**

4   Arnold Schwarzenegger **91**

5   Julia Roberts **106**

TABLES

4.1   Top stars by agency 97

4.2   Top five films at the North American box office 1990–1999 102

CHARTS

4.1   Tom Hanks at the North American box office 1990–1999 104

4.2   Bruce Willis at the North American box office 1990–1999 105

4.3   Julia Roberts at the North American box office 1990–1999 107

ACKNOWLEDGEMENTS

My thanks must go first and foremost to Bridget and Jessica for all their love and support over the years. I would also like to thank my colleagues at the University of Surrey Roehampton, Frank Krutnik and Valarie Lucas, for providing me with valuable information and materials. Finally, thanks to Yoram Allon at Wallflower Press for his patience in believing that a finished manuscript would finally arrive.

INTRODUCTION: LOOKING AT STARS

To speak of stardom in Hollywood as a system is to draw attention to how the American film business has employed, and continues to employ, regular strategies for exploiting star performers in the production and consumption of films. Using the word 'system' immediately invokes ideas of stardom as involving an organised interrelationship of elements or features. To study the star system is to look for the standard mechanisms used by the film industry to construct and promote the images of leading performers.

However, the star system is not directed towards producing a uniform category of star: the star system deals in individualism. In Hollywood, stars are represented to moviegoers as distinctively different people and stardom requires moviegoers to be able to differentiate one performer from another. The star system has therefore developed through the emergence of mechanisms for the production of popular identities.

This book examines the place of stars in cinema and takes an historical approach to the star system in Hollywood. As the star system has become an established feature of Hollywood, cinema stars have attracted a great deal of commentary from many quarters. In the press, reviewers and critics discuss the role of stars when evaluating new film releases. Magazine articles will profile stars in their on- and off-screen lives, constructing for their readership an idea of the star's public and private identity. Interviews appear in the press and on radio and television.

Published biographies can feature in the non-fiction best-seller lists and cause some controversy if exposing hitherto secret aspects of a star's life. All these types of output raise stars to public awareness as part of the ongoing matters of contemporary popular culture.

Outside of popular attention to stars, there has developed a whole body of academic work attempting to understand the social and cultural significance of film stardom. This work has combined many perspectives that has seen stars from the perspectives of economics, sociology and psychology (for overviews of this work see Dyer 1998; McDonald 1995 and 1998). During the 1980s and 1990s, the academic field of film studies in Britain and North America has tended to see stars in the semiotic framework of reading stars as signs or images. This work has developed from Richard Dyer's highly influential book *Stars*, first published in 1979 (revised edition 1998). Reading stars as images involves close analysis of the signs presented by stars on-screen in their performances but also the other texts that relate to the star through publicity and promotions. As this work has developed, it has been the main concern to see how those images can be seen to relate to the social and historical conditions in which they emerge.

At the start of Dyer's book, a distinction is made between stars as a 'phenomenon of production' (a part of the economic control of the film industry) and as a 'phenomenon of consumption' (the meanings represented by stars to audiences). It is characteristic of the book and of the research it has subsequently influenced that the issues arising from the latter are prioritised over the former; when looking at film stars, recent academic study has tended to concentrate on the images of stars without thinking of the industry producing those images. Dyer's work was motivated by the need to explain the popular significance of stars, a work of such complexity that it has deserved considerable attention. The problem with only following this line of study, however, is that it loses sight of where stars come from. As a system, Hollywood stardom is the effect of image and industry.

This book is an attempt to partly redress the imbalance. Here the star system will be explored as a component of the Hollywood film business.

Any study of the star system must combine an understanding of both industry and image. While not ignoring the images of stars, this book does not set out to provide the type of detailed analyses of star images found in recent academic studies. Instead, the emphasis is more on the place of stars in the organisation of the industry and how that industry has set conditions for the production and use of star images. This does not mean displacing the dominance of the semiotic by the economic in the study of stars. Either option on its own is inevitably reductive. Rather it is the concern of this study to explore the conditions that have existed in Hollywood for the making of stars and the images that the system has produced. This is a book therefore about Hollywood and the production of popular star identities: it is concerned both with the business of Hollywood stardom and the production of commercial identities.

Chapter one establishes a basic framework for thinking about the place of stars in the film business as a combination of image, labour and capital. The chapters that follow pick out key phases in the development of the star system in American cinema. Chapter two deals with the place of stars in nineteenth-century American theatre and the factors that led to the emergence of the film star. This is then followed by a discussion of the place of stars in the studio system of the 1930s and 1940s. Finally, the book looks at the transformation of the star system after the studio era and the place of stars in contemporary Hollywood. While each of these chapters describes the general conditions in which the star system operated in these phases, case studies are included to explore in more detail instances of how particular stars or organisations became representative of conditions in the system at that time.

It has been necessary to put emphasis on particular aspects of the star system. For example, chapter three looks at marketing methods and the contracting of stars, while in chapter four the importance of agencies is discussed. This is not intended to suggest that these aspects of the system are only relevant to the phases covered by these chapters but rather to draw attention to where these aspects have a crucial importance in understanding the operations of the system in those contexts. The book relies on drawing together much of the existing published work on the star system. There remain, however, many holes that still need to be filled in the understanding of how stars have operated and continue to operate in the American film industry. It is therefore hoped that this book may provide a foundation to further exploration of the star system.

1   STARDOM AS A SYSTEM

The place of stars in Hollywood cinema can be understood from a number of directions. Stars appear in films and others forms of media texts that cumulatively form the images of stars. At one level, these texts form the general image of Hollywood stardom, the image of stars as wealthy, glamorous and beautiful human beings. At another level, texts are linked by their reference to a single person. Linking texts in this way, the image constructs the star as a particular identity. Stars are not just images. Stars are people who work in the film industry and as such they form a part of the labour force of film production. The role of the star in the industry is not, however, only confined to their function in the process of film-making. In a commercial cinema such as Hollywood, stars are important to the processes of production (making films) but also distribution (selling and marketing films) and exhibition (showing films to paying audiences). Film-making is a high cost and high risk enterprise. Stars are used by the film industry as a means to try and manage audience demand for films. Distributors use the presence of stars to sell films to exhibitors in domestic and overseas markets. Exhibitors, who own and run the theatres showing films, are attracted to films with stars because it is believed the presence of stars help to draw audiences to films. In this circuit of commercial exchange, the star therefore becomes a form of capital, that is to say a form of asset deployed with the intention of gaining advantage in the entertainment market and making profits. This chapter further explores the role of stars as images, labour and capital. In other words, the chapter considers stars as a source of meaning, work and money.

Stars as Images

From the earliest years of the system, the identities of film stars were constructed for commercial purposes across many different sources. It is this construction of identity that Richard Dyer (1998: 34) defines as a star's image:

> By image ... I do not understand an exclusively visual sign, but rather a complex configuration of visual, verbal and aural signs. This configuration may constitute the general image of stardom or of a particular star. It is manifest not only in films but in all kinds of media text.

Dyer sees the images of stars constructed across various categories of texts, including not only a star's film appearances, but also forms of publicity and promotion. Additionally, stars are the objects of critical reviewing and other forms of commentary, for example published star profiles, biographies and interviews. Other factors contributing to the images of stars are the characters they play and the style of performance they use to portray that role. It is also necessary to consider the types of film or genres a star appears in. Stars are also categorised by social variables of age, gender, race and nationality. In semiotic terms, the images of stars are therefore the product of signification. Stars are mediated identities, textual constructions, for audiences do not get the real person but rather a collection of images, words and sounds which are taken to stand for the person. From their familiarity with a range of star texts, moviegoers form impressions of that person so that the star becomes a collection of meanings.

It would be worth adding to Dyer's notion of star image the relevance of gossip, for informal talk about well-known performers is one of the clearest examples of how stars enter into popular culture and everyday life. Frequently a source of unfounded rumour, gossip may depart from the actual truth of stars' lives. Rumour cannot be simply dismissed as falsity however, for if the same untruth is repeated regularly and becomes known by enough people, then rumours can come to define something of the truth of a star's image. Even when it is acknowledged that a particular story about a star is untrue, rumours can still have a residual effect, a legacy, which contributes to the enduring image of that star.

While the identities of stars are highly individuated, Dyer points out that a star is never wholly unique. The images of stars appear both ordinary and extraordinary. Through their images, stars appear ordinary and like other people in society. In this sense stars are not unique because they are typical. Stars are, however, also shown to be exceptional and somehow apart from society. The wealth and looks of stars set them apart from everyday people. It is never possible for any individual member of the audience to comprehensively know all the textual sources through which a star's identity is represented. Knowledge of stars is therefore differently dispersed across society. Moviegoers also bring many different social and cultural competencies to their understanding of a star's identity, so that the image will be interpreted in many different ways. The meaning of a star's image is therefore not contained in the sources that represent the star but is produced in the moment of interaction between moviegoers and star texts.

For this reason, the images of stars are open to a range of differentiated readings. However, this is not to suggest that the meanings of stars is entirely open to individual or subjective interpretation. The images of stars are open to a range of meanings and readings but that range is inevitably limited. At one level, the meaning of star image is constrained by the content of star texts. Jack Nicholson smiles in a particular way. He speaks with a certain rhythm. Opinions may differ over whether Jack Nicholson is charming or vulgar, menacing or sexy, but it seems unlikely that his image will be read as conveying innocence and moral purity.

Equally important is to see star texts in context, to recognise that readings take place in particular cultural and historical circumstances.

One of the most obvious indicators of the historical determination of a star's popularity is the fact that stars seem to be objects of fashion and changing audience tastes. A star who at one time entertained enormous popularity because he or she was seen to be 'of the moment' may very quickly become stale in the public imagination. This cannot be seen as a matter of mere caprice on the part of the audience however, for the fashionability of stars raises questions about what makes a star popular at one time and not another. In certain cases, stars seem to transcend historical fashions, enjoying continued popularity over different periods of time. In such cases, however, the image of a star is nevertheless still historically transformed. The Marilyn Monroe of the 1950s, for example, is not the same as the Monroe of the early twenty-first century.

Stars as Labour

Various developments in Europe and the United States during the nineteenth century led to the invention of moving image technology. Although this prototype film technology was available before this time, the first uses of film as an entertainment medium occurred in the 1890s. In this period, film went from being a technology to a business. The moving image moved from being an object of scientific curiosity to becoming a commodity, a thing that could be sold. It is in this early commercialisation that the moving image can be said to have moved from the status of film, i.e. a strip of photographs, to cinema, i.e. the industry for exploiting the economic value of the image.

Emerging at the end of the nineteenth century, cinema became a product of the changes experienced in various European nations and the United States that had seen those countries become industrial capitalist economies. Cinema itself became a capitalist enterprise. Initially, the cinema industry made money by protecting the patents to camera and projector technology. It would take several years for producers to start regarding the content of films as the main source of revenue for the industry.

In her work on the Hollywood film industry, Janet Staiger (1985b) borrows the Marxist concept of the 'mode of production' to explain the work of film production as a capitalist enterprise. Although Staiger sees the history of the American film industry as the growth of an overarching capitalist mode of production, she identifies different *systems of production*. A system of production is effectively a sub-system of the capitalist mode of production, marked by patterns in the arrangement of labour, technology and capital. During the history of Hollywood, the organisation of the star system has changed as the structure of the film industry as a whole has changed. The changes Staiger describes are discussed in more detail in the following chapters, for they are important in identifying the emergence and subsequent transformation of the star system.

Staiger sees patterns in the organisation of labour as central to identifying transition in systems of production. She regards the labour force in Hollywood as broken down into different categories of workers, for example cameramen and women, scriptwriters, prop-makers, and so on. All these roles represent a particular task in the overall process of making a film. Staiger describes this system as a 'detailed division of labour' (1985b: 91); unlike a social division of labour, in which one worker will be involved in all stages of producing something from first devising to the finished product, a detailed division of labour splits production into a series of separate functions. For Staiger, the arrival of a detailed division of labour in Hollywood was the result of the American film industry increasing the volume of films made, requiring studios to imitate factory-like modes of mass production. Under a detailed division of labour, particular functions become an area of specialisation. Workers perform some tasks and not others. Staiger also points out that the organisation of labour in Hollywood established a hierarchical system, between management and talent or the crafts, and then between the different levels of responsibility and decision making in those areas. As a capitalist industry, Hollywood has therefore organised labour on the structural principles of specialisation and hierarchical power.

Stars fit into this structure. In the division of labour, stars are categorised as performance specialists: stars are required to execute certain tasks. During pre-production, star work involves reading scripts sent to them and the learning of lines. When a film is in production and undertaking principal photography, the star's work requires some limited rehearsal time, the shooting of scenes on location or in the studio, and repeated takes. In post-production, stars will do some dubbing or post-synchronisation of the voice during sound re-recording. For many performers, this will be the end of their work on a film but as stars have an important role to play in the distribution of films, star labour also involves participating in the various promotional tasks of giving press interviews, appearing at gala premieres and appearing on television chat shows.

These are the specialist responsibility of the star in the division of labour. Stars may be categorised as performance specialists but their position in the industry is also marked by their hierarchical status. Not all film actors are stars. In the labour pool of actors, stars are the elite. There is a lot of overlap in the working responsibilities of stars and ordinary performers (learning lines, dubbing, and so on) but also differences. Ordinary performers will not have to complete the promotional commitments that a star will, however a star will not have to undergo the humiliation and disappointment of the auditioning process.

Danae Clark (1995) describes the distinction between stars and ordinary performers in terms of 'labour power differences'. For Clark, any understanding of the star system cannot concentrate exclusively on those performers with star status but must see the star as a relative position in conditions of labour power: 'Though the term "star system" refers to the institutional hierarchy established to regulate and control the employment and use of *all* actors, stars have become a privileged class within the division of actors' labour' (1995: 5; emphasis in original). Seeing the star system in this way demands consideration of the power that attaches to stardom in the film industry.

Stars as Capital

To understand why stars have more power in the film industry than other ordinary performers, it is necessary to see that stars are not just a source of labour but also a form of capital. Stars are valuable to the industry in ways that extend beyond simply how they play a character. After the labour force, Staiger see the other aspects of the capitalist mode of production as the means of production and the mechanisms for financing production. The means of production defines not only the physical resources of buildings, materials and technologies required to make films, but also the skills, knowledge and techniques employed in the use of those resources. Financing in a capitalist mode of production requires the supply of money or capital for the purchase of physical resources and labour. Capitalist industry works as a system by combining labour, technology and capital in ways intended to produce and maximise profits. The products of labour become commodities sold in the market and it has been a classic concern of the critics of capitalism that commodity production separates the product from its creator, with the effect that the labour force is alienated by the organisation of production.

Stars have a place in the film industry both as a category of labour and a form of capital: a star becomes a form of capital because in the commercial film industry, he or she is a valuable asset for a production company. Stars are a form of investment, employed in film productions as a probable guard against loss. The wages of stars account for a major portion of any film's budget and stars are also a marketing tool, whose images are promoted with the intention of trying to effect the entertainment market. Barry King (1987) also points out that stars act as capital because in the contemporary film industry, they have increasingly established their own companies so as to profit from the sale of their images.

Early cinema used brand names to differentiate the products of film production companies. After the arrival of the star system, however, films were increasingly marketed through star differentiation. Cathy Klaprat (1985) sees the value of stars through the economic principles of product differentiation and demand inelasticity. In economics, when demand for any product can be seen to decrease if the price is raised, or to increase if the price is lowered, then the market for a product is said to be elastic. However, where changes in price do not effect demand, the market is inelastic. Klaprat argues that with the most popular performers of the studio era in Hollywood, star differentiation could theoretically stabilise demand, creating a consistent box office performance for a star's films and so allowing distributors to raise the price of their product in dealing with exhibitors. Star differentiation therefore became a valuable strategy in Hollywood, offering a means for not only stabilising the price of films but also the raising of prices for certain products.

While differentiation is crucial to the economic value of stars, rarely have stars ever maintained a consistent record at the box office. Rather than fully accepting Klaprat's view of stars as a mechanism for manipulating the market for films, we can more cautiously suggest that stars act as a means of product differentiation which can only potentially stabilise the market.

Stars do appear to offer an unrivalled opportunity for product differentiation. At one level, various individual stars appear to share common characteristics, and the system of stardom differentiates performers according to type. For example, the young male rebel type is a category which would include stars of the 1950s, like Marlon Brando or James Dean, but also stars of later decades, such as Sean Penn or Christian Slater. At a further level however, the star system seems to resist the classification of stars as types. The identities or images of stars are of value to the film industry for they appear as individuals. Staiger suggests that from an economic point of view, 'stars may be thought of as a monopoly on a personality' (1985b: 101). Monopolies emerge when there is only one supplier to a market. Star monopolies are based on a belief in unique individuality: 'there is only one Jim Carrey'.

The monopoly status of stars is not only of value to producers and distributors. As Leo Rosten observed, star labour has a uniqueness which 'places that personality in an almost unchallengeable bargaining position' (1941: 329). Historical examples have shown that both producers and stars are aware of the value of personal monopoly represented through a star's image. How that monopoly is defined and used is therefore potentially an area for struggle. Star contracts must deal with stars as both labour and capital, defining relationships over not only the star as a particular category of worker but also the star as a property and a product that can be exploited for commercial purposes in image markets.

Star work has a different status in the labour market than other types of work. In manufacturing – for example – labour is hired to produce something separate from the person. The sale of that product as a commodity in the market has been the basis for Marxist arguments that labour is alienated in capitalist economies. At first glance, this condition would not appear to apply to stars, for here the person and the thing produced are one. However, there are potential grounds for division between the star as working person and the star as image, a division between the star as labour and the star as capital. The image may be taken to represent the person but it is also separable from the person. Star images are circulated in various forms of text and in many different contexts. Star contracts must therefore define not only the conditions of an actor's labour but also the rights to use the star's image. As Jane Gaines (1992) observes, the contracts of stars are intended to cover two legal entities: the private person of the performer and the star image.

Gaines points out that star contracts are based on conditions of exclusivity. Unlike other categories of labour, involving the sale of knowledge or skill, the work of stars is based on the selling of a distinctive identity. To sue for breach of contract, the employer must be able to show that a star's services are extraordinary and unique, and that without the services of that particular star, the employer would be damaged in ways that could not be compensated. Equally, the contracts of stars must determine the rights to the exploitation of a star's image. Studying particular examples of star contracts, Gaines sees conditions laid out to determine the right to use a star's 'acts, poses, plays and appearances', and then the 'name, voice and likeness' of the star (1992: 157). The former appear as part of a feature film and as such are the property of the film's copyright holder. The second, however, can be used to carry the star's image into other media, designed for commercial and promotional use.

Gaines comments that 'there is more at stake in the enforcement of a personal services contract in the entertainment industry than in other fields of employment because the entertainer *is* the product' (1992: 153; emphasis in original). The relationship of person to image is the ground

13

for potential legal conflict for the star system. While the star has some control over how he or she appears on-screen, depending on the agreed terms, contracts can grant the right to use a star's name, voice or likeness in ways which may not be seen to be desirable to the star as a person. The image is therefore always liable to escape the individual control of the star.

The Production of Popular Identities

There are several connections to be made between seeing the star as image, labour and capital. Star images are collections of meanings read from various star texts. Star work involves the labour of contributing to the creation of some of those texts. In the Hollywood industry, stars are placed in the structure of specialised and hierarchically organised relationships with other categories of labour. Unlike other performers, stars have greater power in the industry because of their dual capacity as labour *and* capital. The star becomes a form of capital inasmuch as his or her image can be used to create advantage in the market for films and secure profits. Because the image is not the person but rather a set of texts and meanings that signify the person, then the image is something separable from the star. Star contracts cover both the labour of the star but also the product of that labour, the image. Contracts set out the ownership and control of the image, defining who has the right to use the image, or parts of the image, and in what contexts. The images of stars are therefore legal entities.

What follows is an attempt to explore these connections between stars as image, labour and capital during different phases of Hollywood history. We will look at the place of the star system in the changing conditions of the industry as a whole but also how examples of particular cases, be they stars or organisations, represent certain trends in the system at that time.

2   MAKING THE SYSTEM

When tracing the foundations of the film star system, some histories of the cinema have frequently repeated a now familiar anecdote as the catalytic moment for the creation of the system (see, for example, Cook 1996: 40; Jacobs 1968: 86–7). The story goes something like this. In the first decade of the twentieth century, American film production companies withheld the names of film performers, despite requests from audiences, fearing that public recognition would drive performers to demand higher salaries. This policy was followed by the powerful companies of the Motion Picture Patents Company (MPPC) (i.e. Biograph, Edison, Essanay, Kalem, Kleine Optical, Lubin, Pathé Frères, Selig Polyscope, Star Film and Vitagraph) and independent producers and distributors. In 1910, however, the independent producer Carl Laemmle directly confronted the power of the MPPC when he lured the leading Biograph actor Florence Lawrence to his company, the Independent Motion Picture (IMP) Corporation (later the Universal studio). Laemmle promoted Lawrence's arrival at IMP by naming her in an elaborate piece of newspaper publicity. On 12 March, Laemmle bought space in the trade paper *Moving Picture World* to denounce a previous story supposedly run by a St Louis newspaper which had allegedly reported that Lawrence, previously known only as 'The Biograph Girl', was killed in a car accident. Proclaiming 'We nail a lie', the IMP announcement named Lawrence as the new 'IMP girl' and reassured readers of the actor's continued good health and her forthcoming appearance in *The Broken Bath*, to be released on 14 March.

While the anecdote is appealing for its portrayal of Laemmle's entrepreneurial cheek and the courageous struggle it conjures up of a nascent independent fighting the mighty MPPC, it does not satisfactorily account for how the star system emerged in American cinema. Recent accounts of the film star system have seen cause to revise this conventional history. While film actors were not named in early cinema, there is evidence to show that producers were advertising the names of leading performers prior to the Lawrence incident. A further difficulty with the story is that it tends to imply that the star system was the invention of the early film industry. American theatre, however, had already formed its own star system during the nineteenth century, providing an example to the film industry of the value in promoting individual fame for the entertainment business.

To examine these foundations further, this chapter looks at the impact of the star system on nineteenth-century American theatre before tracing the earliest actions by the film industry to name and promote its leading actors.

American Theatre and the Coming of the Star System

Before the War of American Independence (1775–1781), companies of British actors toured the colonies of the 'New World'. Professional theatre began in America during 1752 when the London manager William Hallam organised a group of ten actors led by his brother Lewis. The Hallam company took up residence in Williamsburg, Virginia, performing a repertory of plays by established English dramatists, including Shakespeare and Farquhar (see Harris 1994).

Lacking the prestige of the legitimate English theatre, the colonial companies were unable to attract the best acting talent and certainly not the stars of the London stage (see Mordden 1981). Instead, Hallam employed his wife and other members of his family, and the company came to represent the stock system that continued to dominate American theatre until the late nineteenth century. Based on the recollections of family member Lewis Hallam Jr., the theatre historian William Dunlap described the Hallam company as 'a well organised republic, every member of which had his part assigned to him, both private and public, behind and before the curtain' (1832: 509). In the stock company, a group of actors would be employed for a season to specialise in playing characters cast by familiar 'lines of business' or types of role, for example 'leading man/lady', 'heavy', 'soubrette' or 'old woman' (McArthur 1984: 5–7). Salaries would be scaled according to these lines of business. Built on the principle of ensemble playing, the stock company system did not privilege the appearance of individual star performers.

While indigenous companies were in existence at the end of the eighteenth century, even after independence the English stage continued to dominate the theatre in North America. During the early nineteenth century, centres of theatre culture were established along the eastern seaboard. Following an increase of population and wealth in urban centres, major theatre houses were established in Philadelphia, New York and Charleston, and tours of America began to appear more attractive to leading actors from London. In 1810, the English tragedian George Frederick Cooke became the first star of the London stage to tour America. Cooke's visit started a trend which saw English stars touring theatres to appear for a few performances in leading roles supported by resident stock company actors (see Wilson 1966).

Amongst the English stars to follow Cooke's example was the famous Shakespearean actor, Edmund Kean. After an unremarkable and often difficult career as a strolling player, Kean came to star prominence in London when in 1814 he took the role of Shylock in 'The Merchant of Venice' at Drury Lane. Kean's status was largely due to his style of acting, which became well known for its dynamic energy and violent emotionality. As the English critic William Hazlitt observed, 'Kean is all effort, all violence, all extreme passion; he is possessed with a fury, a demon that leaves him no repose, no time for thought or room for imagination' and Samuel Coleridge famously remarked, 'to see Kean was to read Shakespeare by flashes of lightning' (both quoted in Cole and Chinoy 1970: 327). Motivated by financial difficulties he was having in Britain at the time, Kean first visited America in 1820, appearing in New York,

Philadelphia and Boston to perform a repertory of Shakespearean roles, including Hamlet, Othello and Richard III. For his appearances, Kean was paid £50 for each performance, plus a share of box-office profits (see Taubman 1967). Kean later returned in 1825 for a second tour.

Cooke and Kean represented the influence of the English star system on the American theatre. For certain commentators, the dominance of the American theatre scene by the London stage was a cause for nationalistic outrage. For example, the American poet Walt Whitman declared that 'English managers, English actors, and English plays ... must be allowed to die away among us, as usurpers of our stage' (quoted in Taubman 1967: 83). American theatre began to find its first crop of indigenous theatre stars from the 1820s through to the 1850s. Notable names of the period were Edwin Forrest, Mary Ann Duff, Charlotte Cushman and Edwin Booth, among others.

With the appearance of these early indigenous stars, some commentators were critical of what they saw as the influence of popular performers on American theatre. Writing in his autobiography, the theatre manager William B. Wood saw the advent of stars as a consequence of broader social changes, a symptom of nineteenth-century modernity brought about by 'a spirit of change – of exhilaration – of excitement, incident to an end of an old order of things, and the advent of some new and undefined ones' (Wood 1855: 544). Wood lamented the effect of stars on the American stage, believing 'regular actors no longer form ... a stock company, but [are] reduced to the condition of mere ministers or servants upon some principal performer, whose attractions it was now their sole and chief duty to increase, illustrate, or set off'. Wood's observations were prophetic, forecasting the trend that would bring sweeping changes to the American theatre in the second half of the nineteenth century.

While the American theatre saw its own native stars emerge during the nineteenth century, for most of the century the theatre remained dominated by the stock company system. During the 1870s however, the stock system began to decline. As a result of railroad building during the civil war, large-scale theatrical tours became easier and affordable (Harris 1994: 7). Combination companies, as they were known, were brought together for a single play instead of a season of plays. Where the stock actor was hired to perform a special line of business across a series of plays, actors in the combination system were employed to perform a specific role in a single play. To support the economics of the combination system, managers and booking agents assumed a new importance in the planning of major tours, and star names were marketed to sell tours around the national circuit.

In the last decades of the nineteenth century, the decline in the stock company system and domination of the combination company was central to fully instituting a star system in American theatre. By the time of the arrival of cinema in the mid-1890s therefore, American theatre already offered a representative model of the economic and symbolic importance of stars in popular entertainment.

Case Study: Edwin Forrest, the Bowery B'hoys and the Declaration of American Stardom

Edwin Forrest made his professional debut in 1820 at the age of fourteen, and developed a career based on his passionate portrayal of great tragic roles. Forrest enjoyed mass appeal with his native audience and has come to occupy a place in theatre history as the first home-grown American star. With his agile physique and sonorous voice, Forrest was well known for his energetic performance style. Like Kean, to whom Forrest played a supporting role during the English star's 1825 tour, Forrest's stardom depended on the dynamic and aggressive spectacle of his acting. Early in his career, Forrest became associated with the Bowery Theatre (opened in 1826), situated in one of the tougher areas of New York, where his vibrant acting style won him a loyal audience amongst the local 'Bowery B'hoys'.

Although frequently likened to Kean, Forrest's acting assumed nationalistic significance as the mark of an American style and tradition. For Walt Whitman, reviewing Forrest's performance as 'The Gladiator' for an 1846 edition of the *Brooklyn Eagle*, the star displayed a distinctive American style. While Whitman praised Forrest's performances, he saw the star's style eagerly imitated but rarely equalled by the many other actors of the day who chose to adopt a 'loud mouthed ranting style' (Whitman 1846: 546). Forrest's national significance was most pronounced during the 1849 tour by the English star, William Charles Macready. In contrast to the passion of Forrest, Macready worked with a far more restrained acting style.

When Forrest performed in London during 1845, he received a hostile reception from British audiences, a response which the American star believed was maliciously cultivated by Macready. Disputes between Forrest and Macready escalated during the English actor's 1849 tour of America, culminating in scenes of public disorder. When Macready appeared as Macbeth at the Astor Place Theatre on 8 May, the Bowery B'hoys disrupted the performance with shouting, heckling and the throwing of chairs onto the stage. Returning to the Astor two days later, Macready was once again subjected to a hostile reception. As the house became more rowdy, the night turned into a full scale riot, ending when an infantry unit fired into the crowd, killing twenty-two people and injuring many others (Taubman 1967: 89–92). In retrospect, the Astor Place Riot appears as more than simply a conflict between two actors. Forrest was not just a star but an *American* star. Forrest's stardom represented not only the popular appeal of a single performer but also a wider sense of American theatre struggling to break from a colonial past and produce its own cultural identity.

Early Film – Cinema without Stars

While the star system was firmly established in the American theatre by the end of the nineteenth century, early cinema did not immediately emulate the theatre business. Film technology was developed in various contexts at the end of the century. In the United States, Thomas Edison and William Kennedy Laurie Dickson developed the Kinetoscope camera, which Edison patented in 1891, followed by the Kinetograph viewing machine. The Kinetograph allowed one person at a time to watch short films or Kinetophones. In Europe, machines were developed for the projection of large images to a public audience. In 1895, the French brothers Auguste and Louis Lumière patented their Cinématographe, a combined camera, printer and projector. That same year the German brothers Max and Émile Skladanowsky patented the Bioskop projector, and in Britain, Robert W. Paul and partner Birt Acres built their own camera, which Paul accompanied with a commercial patent in 1896 for his projector, the Theatrograph.

In this immediate phase of early cinema, business was driven by the economics of film hardware. The first film companies were the patent holders and manufacturers of camera and projection equipment. These manufacturers regarded the technological display of moving images in itself to be the prime appeal for audiences. The films themselves were of secondary concern and early cinema was marketed to audiences through the exciting possibilities of film technology. This trend marked a departure from the theatre, which was dominated by the production of narrative dramas. Tom Gunning (1986) regards early film-makers of the period 1895–1906 as developing what he calls a 'cinema of attractions'. Excited by the technological possibilities of projecting moving pictures, film-makers created a cinema of attractions which explored the wide range of uses for film to record and *show* something. Early films frequently worked to document a real-life moment and, in some cases, film-makers would manipulate the technology so as to transform reality. For example, the Lumières' *Démolition d'un Mur* (*Falling Wall*) (1895) documented the knocking down of a wall into a pile of rubble followed by the use of reverse printing to create the magical illusion of the wall returning to the former upright and intact state. This preoccupation was different to that of narrative cinema, in which film was explored as a medium specifically to *represent* a fictional world. Early cinema was not without narrative fictions and the Lumières would also make the two actor comedy short *L'Arroseur Arrosé* (*The Gardener and the Bad Boy*) (1895).

Early film-makers were therefore not concerned exclusively with making non-narrative films but the entertainment appeal of dramas or story films did not lead the business thinking of the industry at this time. By perceiving the value of the medium to be in the attraction of film technology, the early cinema business did not immediately look towards copying the practices of the theatre, including the star system. Reflecting on early film history, it could be argued that the first stars of cinema were the camera and the projector; however this would be erroneous, for it would be to miss the point that the early film business in the United States and Europe developed as a cinema without a need for stars.

While acknowledging that cinema emerged as a medium of show rather than a medium of drama, it is important, however, not to lose sight of what was shown in early films. Although technology was the draw for audiences of the period, early films also immediately reveal the preoccupation amongst film-makers with recording the activities of human subjects. Working in Edison's studio, known as the 'Black Maria', Dickson created numerous shorts, including films with descriptive titles such as *Blacksmith Scene* (1893), *Record of a Sneeze* (1894), *Amateur Gymnast* (1894) and *The Barbershop* (1894) (see Musser 1994). In the Lumière brothers' famous *La Sortie des Ouvriers de L'usine Lumière* (*Workers Leaving the Lumière Factory*) (1895), the static camera captures people in an everyday ritual. The attraction of early cinema therefore combined a fascination with the spectacle of technology and the spectacle of human action. It is this showing of people on screen which has made cinema from its earliest moment a performance medium if not exclusively a dramatic medium.

The type of performance created by early cinema was not orientated towards the construction of star identities. Where film-makers did produce short narratives, the presentation of human subjects excluded elements essential to screen stardom. It was the convention of early narrative film-making to anchor the camera in a fixed position that set the action in a long shot at a distance from where it was difficult to recognise or individuate the actors. Without credits to identify the names of the actors or the characters they played, the performers of early narrative cinema were undistinguished and unknown.

In some cases, short films were made of performers who already enjoyed a reputation in other fields of entertainment. Between 1896–1906, early cinema was organised around a period of itinerant exhibition, as projectionists travelled with their equipment and films to show as inserts in vaudeville programmes (Allen 1980). The interaction of cinema and vaudeville extended to the cast of performers who appeared in early films. In March 1894, Dickson filmed the Austrian strongman, Eugene Sandow. Other names from the vaudeville stage featured in Kinetograph shorts, including the Spanish dancer Carmencita, contortionist Madame Edna Bertoldi, facial contortionist George Layman, and boxing duo the Glenroy Brothers (Musser 1994). Running for less than a minute, these shorts showed extracts from longer stage acts. One Kinetograph subject, the vaudeville dancer Annabelle Moore, caused a scandal when she was rumoured to have danced naked at a New York stag party given by the showman P. T. Barnum. Although the incident was denied, copies of her film *Annabelle Dancing* increased in price from $10 to $40 (see Christie 1994).

With dancers and contortionists as its subject matter, the look of early cinema was drawn to the attraction of seeing the movement and manipulation of the human body. For Gunning, the cinema of attractions was an *exhibitionist* cinema, creating a spectacle that self-consciously acknowledged the presence of the audience, against the *voyeuristic* cinema of narrative film in which the audience spy on a framed world that does not appear aware of the spectator. Dickson's films of vaudeville performers were representative of this exhibitionist tendency. Subjects were filmed in such a way that they performed direct to camera, reproducing the presentational address of the popular stage. With Sandow, the camera captured the strongman in medium long shot as he flexed and displayed his musculature to the camera. In early cinema, therefore, the performers who appeared on screen were professionals from outside the cinema, and the look of the camera demonstrated a greater preoccupation with the show of bodies over the representation of dramatic characters.

The Emergence of the Film Actor

While early film brought performers such as Sandow and Carmencita to the attention of film audiences, in the first years of the twentieth century the American cinema did not have a star system. For vaudeville performers, any degree of public recognition they enjoyed was for the work they did outside the cinema. Vaudeville acts did not perform regularly enough in film to construct any substantial cinematic fame. Also early producers or exhibitors did not seek to market films through the names of performers. Films were shot in such ways that actors could not be clearly identified and audiences had no means of knowing the individuals who appeared on screen. It was the predominant mode of early cinema therefore to present anonymous bodies on screen.

Three factors appear central to the development of the star system in the American cinema. First, the industrial organisation of film-making based on systems of mass production in the United States and the move towards a specialised or detailed division of labour involved in this process. Secondly, growth in the production of narrative film and the formal changes in the organisation of on-screen space that resulted from this change. Finally, the beginnings of an active circulation of information about the identities of performers in films.

In early cinema, small film companies comprised a handful of individuals creating product for the projection technicians who ran itinerant exhibition. As changes in the organisation of film distribution, exhibition and production saw the scale of business grow, then cinema became a fully fledged industry (see Balio 1985a). From 1903, film exchanges opened enabling cost effective distribution and a regular supply of new releases to exhibitors. Increased audience demand led to the boom from 1904–5 in the building of small nickelodeon storefront theatres. As thousands of small storefront theatres opened between 1907–1909, the American film business stepped up film-making activity, gradually moving towards an industrial model of mass production. The period 1907–1913 saw a shift in the geography of film production as companies moved towards the west coast of the United States to take advantage of the warmer climate and brighter shooting conditions. The concentration of production facilities in and around a single Los Angeles suburb has meant that since this time the American film industry is frequently referred to simply as Hollywood. It was in the context of this industrialisation of the American film business that the star system would eventually emerge.

With an increase in the volume of film production, the American industry saw the transition from what Janet Staiger (1985b) sees as the organisation of production centred on the cameraman to a director-led system of production. At Edison, Dickson was representative of the cameraman system, taking overall responsibility not only to photograph a scene, but also to choose the subject matter, stage the performers, and then develop and edit the material. As early as 1904, companies began using directors to manage production and for Staiger the director system was prevalent by 1907. Several directors came to film after experience in the theatre, including D. W. Griffith who joined Biograph in 1907 as a film actor and story writer before becoming a director. With the director system, film-making began to move away from the social division of labour that the cameraman system was based on and towards a detailed division of labour, separating the conception and execution of production with the director managing a crew who individually took responsibility for separate crafts in film-making.

This transition to a detailed division of labour in film production changed the status of the film actor. Before 1907, the performers in early film narratives where either non-professionals or actors who worked in the theatre but took occasional employment in the films (see Musser 1986). Production schedules were irregular and, with films hiring actors for single days, very few performers found regular employment in films. Eileen Bowser (1990) suggests that at this time film was seen to attract those actors from the lower ranks of the profession who were looking for work between engagements. Theatre continued to provide the main source of employment for actors, defining the legitimate working context of the performing professional. While producers feared that naming could give performers wider public recognition, leading to greater power in the negotiation of their contracts, the anonymity of film acting also served the interests of actors who did not want their name associated with the less prestigious work of appearing in films.

From 1907, however, an increase in narrative production provided opportunities for actors to find regular work in films. Producers formed their own equivalent of the stock company system of nineteenth-century theatre, with Vitagraph and other companies hiring a pool of actors who were employed in various roles across a series of films. Paid by the day, leading actors received $10, rank and file players $5, and extras between $2 to $3 (see Balio 1985a). Benjamin McArthur (1984) suggests actors were drawn to working in films, attracted by the money, the widespread exposure and the permanence of their performance recorded on film. Furthermore, Bowser (1990) argues that the regular employment of the screen cowboy Gilbert M. 'Broncho Billy' Anderson and comedian Ben Turpin made these actors the first movie stars. Although actors of the legitimate theatre were hired to appear in films, in many cases the transition from stage to screen proved to be unsuccessful. Stage stars such as the musical-comedy performer Blanche Ring and comedian Eddie Foy Jr. found their work did not translate from live stage to silent screen (see McArthur 1984). The Triangle Studio closed as a result of hiring major stage names on high salaries for films which failed at the box office. Although film struggled against theatrical tradition for recognition of professional legitimacy, the growing film market provided a context in which actors could reasonably expect to work regularly and for comparatively good rates of pay. With industrialisation and the organisation of production through a detailed division of roles, the film actor emerged as a separate category of labour.

It was not only the increased volume of film production that gave actors greater opportunities for work in film at this time but also the growing dominance of narrative production over other types of film and this increase in narrative film production is a second significant factor in the making of the star system in American cinema. Early cinema had taken the novelty of film technology as the basis for its business; however, the attractions of that technology were limited. To maintain demand, the film business saw a shift from prioritising the economics of film hardware towards the concern with driving the market through producing new and attractive films. Before 1903, various types of film appeared in vaudeville programmes. Audiences were offered a wide variety of films, including not only the recordings of vaudeville acts discussed earlier, but also trick films (exploiting the manipulative effects of camera technology), various forms of documentary, comedies and short dramas.

Of the films made in 1904, Robert Allen (1980) sees films with documentary subject matter accounting for forty-two per cent of the total films produced. Comedies comprised forty-five per cent of films, with dramatic narratives accounting for eight per cent and trick films five per cent. Between 1907–1908, a significant change occurred as production of narrative forms in the shape of comedies and dramas swiftly overwhelmed documentary forms. In 1907, production was divided between sixty-seven per cent comedies and dramas, against thirty-three per cent documentaries. By 1908, the imbalance in output had increased to ninety-six per cent narrative forms and only four per cent documentary forms.

There is no clear evidence to suggest why this change should have happened. Allen suggests that the growth in nickelodeon building created an increased demand for new films that required producers to rethink their production practices. Documentary forms required shooting on location, which was not only costly but also placed crews in environments where happenings did not occur under the total control of the crew and so could not be planned or predicted. Narrative production, either in the form of comedies or dramas, could be planned, contained and organised in the controlled environment of the studio, with material generated specifically for that purpose. Allen therefore speculates that the increased volume of narrative film-making came from the need to regularise production in order to supply exhibitors: narrative allowed film-makers and distributors to efficiently control supply to meet demand. While this argument may be a point for further research in film history, it is the effect and not the cause which is important for the star system. Relying on the skilled performer, the increased output of comedies and dramas expanded the labour market for professional actors to work regularly in film.

As film in the United States moved from a cinema of attractions to a narrative cinema, film-makers explored the possibilities of film form in telling stories. Early narrative film-making tended to photograph an entire scene in a single shot, with the camera set at sufficient distance from the action so as to capture the whole body of a performer in long shot. This manner of filming made the frame equivalent to the proscenium arch in the theatre. Like stage actors, a film actor had to be conscious of how he or she placed the body in performance. Film performers were required to keep their bodies at angles that were constantly open to the look of the imaginary audience represented by the fixed camera. Early narrative film therefore displayed a frontal style of performance, limiting the performance possibilities of actors. Filming actors in long shot, these tableaux scenes not only demanded a highly gestural and demonstrative style of acting but also set members of the audience at a distance that prevented the intimate identification necessary for stars to become a recognisable feature of film narrative.

Janet Staiger (1985a) sees the American film industry undergoing a number of changes in the development in narrative film production between 1908–1912. During this period the industry moved more towards character-centred narratives with dialogue intertitles. In a change to film style, the camera was moved closer to the action, cutting actors off at the knees and, on occasions, framing the actor from head to waist in medium shot. As the conventions of continuity editing were elaborated, so an increased use of close-ups, patterns of shot/reverse shot cutting, and eyeline matching, were all used to bring further emphasis to the actor's face as a source of meaning. Changes in staging methods therefore established a complex performance space on screen in which the camera shifted its relationship to the bodies of performers.

With this new performance space came a more physically reserved style of acting. Towards the end of the nineteenth century, American theatre had already seen many actors moving away from the declamatory style of acting associated with melodrama, preferring a more restrained style of playing which was seen to introduce a new standard of realism in acting. Roberta Pearson (1992) identifies a similar shift occurring in American film in the period after narrative film forms began to dominate production. The effects of this transition became most evident in the years 1910–1911. As the use of camera more closely explored the details of the actor's performance, so actors drew on small gestures and facial expressions. This combination of film form and performance style constructed a greater sense of interiority in performance. In the trade papers of the period, commentators viewed this change as bringing psychological complexity to film acting.

Pearson argues this transition played an important part in raising the cultural status of cinema in America. The new acting style was not simply a product of the change in film form but an imitation of the stylistic practices found in the legitimate theatre, signifying a sense of 'quality'. Performance style therefore played a role in distinguishing narrative film from the cinema's roots in vaudeville exhibition. As Pearson comments, 'the shift in performance style can ... be seen as part of cinema's transition from the cheap amusement of the "lower orders" to mainstream medium appealing to patrons of all classes' (1992: 139).

The Discourses of Stardom

While the industrialisation of film production created a detailed division of labour, providing regular employment for actors, and the dominance of narrative production elaborated methods of staging that provided audiences with a more intimate image of performers, these were only necessary but not sufficient conditions for the production of star identities. Audiences could see performers but they had no means of knowing *who* they watched. A final factor in the making of the film star system therefore came with the circulation of information that identified and promoted the images of individual performers. For Richard de Cordova (1990), the emergence of the star system in American cinema came after 1907 with the distribution of certain types of knowledge or 'discourse' about film performers. As film acting became a stable profession, during 1907 the trade press began to publish articles examining the work of the film actor. De Cordova sees the appearance of such articles as marking an important early stage in the emergence of the star system. By making known the work of film acting, these early articles raised public awareness of the human labour involved in the production of on-screen performances, resulting in what he has referred to as the 'discourse on acting'. In line with the transition to a detailed division of labour, in which actors became a specialised category of worker, the discursive construction of the 'film actor' as a category of artistic professional was introduced to the movie-going public. The effect of this discourse was that while individual actors remained unknown, something of the work of acting was revealed.

As cinema matured as an entertainment business in America, members of the MPPC and independent producers marketed their films through brand names. For example, films were sold as Biographs or Vitagraphs. Brand names worked by selling a film through its sameness to other films, offering audiences a reassuring indicator of quality which, as Bowser argues, guaranteed 'uniformity of the product manufactured' (1990: 103). Branding identified one body of films as the work of a particular studio while also differentiating those films from the products of other studios. A brand name was therefore a sign of similarity and difference.

Although branding as a marketing strategy directed the consuming interests of audiences towards the production company and not the performers, when the companies did begin to publish the names of their players, those names functioned in the same way to signify similarity and difference. Early cases of naming occurred before the infamous Laemmle/ Lawrence incident. When Vitagraph, a member of the MPPC, released its production of *Oliver Twist* in May 1909, the film carried an on-screen credit announcing 'Miss Elita Proctor Otis as "Nancy Sykes"' at the point where the actor first appeared in the film. At the same time, the *New York Dramatic Mirror* named Otis and promoted her appearance as Nancy Sykes. Naming personalities worked in conjunction with the new performance space of narrative film to individuate performers. Audiences could begin not only to recognise performers but also have a name to put to the face. As that face and name appeared across films, so an on-screen identity was pieced together.

Further instances of naming soon followed. Edison ran articles on performers in the company's own *Kinetogram* periodical. In particular, the French pantomime artist Pilar-Morin was promoted across a number of films, with the effect that her name became the means for the identification of a specific on-screen identity. It is this use of the name to construct knowledge of performers across a series of film appearances that de Cordova sees as central to advancing the promotion of the 'picture personality'. Where the discourse on acting constructed a supra-individual knowledge of film performance as a craft practised by many, the picture personality introduced a specifically individual knowledge of the single performer.

Naming sectioned off certain performers as worthy of special attention and American cinema began to systematically promote individual actors as a means of marketing films. In particular, Kalem, Edison, and the French company Pathé, all actively announced the names of actors in their films. To promote personalities, production companies introduced new methods for raising awareness of leading names. Alongside newspaper articles and advertisements, the names of actors appeared on lobby cards made by producers for exhibitors to display in theatres, together with slides of favourite actors to be shown between films (see Staiger 1983). Performers made personal appearances and fan magazines were published. By May 1911, the Edison company had started to provide on-screen credits for its actors. Within two years after the first naming of film actors, cinema had discovered many of the basic promotional tools still used to sell stars today.

For de Cordova, the name of the performer was central to the intertextuality of the picture personality's image. At one level, the name functioned to construct the picture personality as an on-screen identity, linking performances in separate films: 'Personality existed as an effect of ... the representation of character across a number of films' (1990: 86). The effect of the name extended beyond the screen, however, into stories carried by the press and fan magazines, yet de Cordova sees this extra-filmic discourse limited to discussion of the on-screen work and roles of personalities. For this reason, knowledge of personalities remained anchored in the performer's on-screen life, with the identities of personalities defined in terms of 'a professional existence – a history of appearances in films and plays and a personality gleaned from those appearances' (p. 92).

While the personality discourse was an important stage in the emergence of the star system, for de Cordova the system itself was only fully realised after 1913 when stories circulated in the press about the off-screen lives of popular film performers. This new realm of knowledge introduced readers to life behind the screen, so that the star was known not only through his or her roles but also as 'a character in a narrative quite separable from his or her work in any film' (p. 99). By combining knowledge of on-screen and off-screen lives, star discourse constructed both a professional and private existence for performers. In the star discourse, de Cordova identifies a central concern with distinguishing the moral healthiness of work in cinema against life in theatre. Compared to the night-time work, travelling and general insecurities of the theatre, working in films was represented as offering regular daytime conditions conducive to maintaining stable domestic and familial lives.

Another set of concerns with the private existence of film performers came through reporting the wealthy lifestyles enjoyed by stars. With big homes and expensive cars, the lifestyle of stars exemplified the values of the consumer economy. Stardom and consumerism both share an element of fantasy and desire. Consumerism is escapist, promoting the fantasy of living beyond basic necessities. The market suggests consumers are free to choose what they want rather than what they need. Through the exercise of choice, consumption takes on the appearance of an act of individual self-expression. Advertising becomes a vital component of the consumer economy, using the image of things to stimulate desire. Images of wealth, freedom and individualism are therefore fundamental to consumerism and since the start of the star system, popular film performers have played a significant role in promoting those values.

With many stars known to have come from humble backgrounds, the glorification of consumption in the coverage of star lifestyles presented the trappings of stardom as material pleasures which could be legitimately aspired to and possibly achieved by one and all. As Lary May observes in his discussion of press reporting on the lifestyles of Douglas Fairbanks and Mary Pickford, 'they demonstrated how modern consumption allowed one to emulate the styles of the high and mighty' (1980: 145–6).

By representing the moral rectitude of performers' lives, star discourse promoted the image of the whole cinema business. Through controlling what became known about a star's private existence, production companies could actively manage the image of the industry, protecting it against those critics who were eager to dismiss cinema as morally degraded and in need of censorial intervention. With many early stars playing on-screen roles as virtuous heroes and heroines whose moral course withstood whatever challenges were put in its way, the representation of a wholesome off-screen existence achieved moral closure between the star's on-screen and off-screen images. During the early 1920s however, newspaper stories began to appear which disrupted that closure. Between 1920–1921, several stories broke about the divorces of stars such as Conway Tearle, Clara Kimbell Young, Francis X. Bushman and Douglas Fairbanks (see de Cordova 1990). Initially, these stories received little attention by the press. From late-1921, however, a series of high profile scandals made headlines and had a profound effect on star discourse. Most notable was the case of popular comedian Roscoe 'Fatty' Arbuckle, who was accused but later acquitted of murdering the film actor Virginia Rappe in his hotel room. For de Cordova, the star scandal added a further level of knowledge to star discourse: 'Exposés on the real lives of the stars would no longer be limited to stories of success, security, and marital bliss; transgression, betrayal, restlessness, and loss entered into the dramatic formula' (1990: 121).

For the early star system, the effect of reporting scandal therefore drew attention to the contradictions that could exist in the images and lives of stars. Through the circulation of the discourses of stardom, audiences came to know who they watched on screen. With the construction of the picture personality, the performer became a vital means of branding and differentiating the film product. Covering the lifestyles of performers, star discourse picked out certain film actors as worthy of identification and desire. In contradiction to what appeared in films and sanctioned accounts of the star's lifestyle, star scandal made known what appeared to be the most intimate truths of a star's identity. Whether true or not, scandal stories were nevertheless important to an audience's understanding of the star as not only an object of desire but also a desiring subject.

Case Study: Mary Pickford – from 'the Girl with the Curls' to United Artists

Mary Pickford holds a significant place in the early history of film stardom. Not only was she one of the most popular stars of the silent era but through her own actions, she effectively exploited her image and in so doing revealed the early value placed by the American film industry on the star as capital. Born in Toronto, real name Gladys Mary Smith, Pickford was still a child when she entered the theatre by joining a local stock company. Her theatrical career continued into her early teens, touring and working for David Belasco in New York, until in 1909 she left the theatre to become a film actor at Biograph under the direction of D. W. Griffith.

It was during her years at Biograph that Pickford achieved her star status. Like all actors of the time, Pickford's appearances for Biograph were uncredited. Pickford can, however, be seen as one of the first players to be lifted out of anonymity by the discourse of the picture personality. In her first big hit for Biograph, Griffith's *The Little Teacher* (1909), intertitles identified Pickford as 'Little Mary', a label that would stick for much of her early film career. Other sources referred to her as 'Goldilocks', 'The Girl with the Curls' and, after Florence Lawrence left for IMP, 'The Biograph Girl'. As Molly Haskell suggests, Pickford's image was similar to that of Griffith's other major female star of the period, Lillian Gish, a type who represented 'the diminutive child-woman' (1987: 58). Pickford's image contrasted sharply with that of other female contemporaries, such as the vampish Theda Bara and the sophisticated Louise Brooks.

Although Pickford's image signified fragility and innocence, the star showed herself to be a shrewd businesswoman, and she was quick to take control of her career. Naming made Pickford into a marketable personality and the value of the star's image was not only recognised and exploited by the studios but also by the star herself. Leaving Biograph to join IMP in December 1910, Pickford successfully negotiated a salary rise to $175 dollars a week. There followed a series of rapid career moves, with a four picture contract the following year at Majestic for $275 a week, and in 1912 a lucrative new contract with Biograph (see Balio 1976).

During a brief return to the Broadway stage in 1913, Pickford was spotted by Adolph Zukor who asked her to join his Famous Players Company. While working for Zukor, Pickford's salary would rise dramatically. Initially signing for $500 a week, Pickford used her name to negotiate ever higher salaries, rising quickly to $1,000 and then $2,000 a week. When the American Film Company offered Pickford $4,000 a week for the serial *The Diamond in the Sky*, Zukor was forced to meet the price to hold on to the star. Such was the value of the Pickford name that Mary's sister Lotte was employed for the series instead. To keep Pickford, Zukor agreed in 1916 to the formation of the star's own production company, The Mary Pickford Corporation, with Pickford owning a 50% interest, taking half the profits of all films and earning $10,000 a week, a guaranteed salary of at least $1 million over two years.

Pickford was able to exercise leverage in salary negotiations for it was known that Paramount, the distributor of films from Famous Players, used the Pickford name to sell packages of films to exhibitors through the practice of block booking (that is, organising sales of fixed packages of film titles that mixed average or poor product with star titles). As Zukor raised Pickford's salary, he passed the cost on to the exhibitor, increasing the guarantee fee from $35,000 to $65,000 and then $120,000. When Pickford's salary went up to $10,000 a week, the guarantee fee reached $165,000 (Pickford 1956). After her contract expired in 1918, First National poached Pickford with an offer of $675,000 for three films, with fifty per cent of profits along with authority to select scripts and the right to have a say in the final cut of her films (Balio 1976).

If Pickford's business acumen contrasted with the image of 'Little Mary', then so did her private life. Initially married to Owen Moore when both were acting at Biograph, the marriage collapsed amidst Moore's drunkenness and Pickford's affair with fellow screen idol, Douglas Fairbanks. In the press, an image of marital bliss was conveyed, working to achieve moral closure between the on-screen and off-screen lives of Pickford. Divorce from Moore in 1920 and Pickford's subsequent marriage to Fairbanks could have fractured that closure. De Cordova observes, however, that Pickford's life neatly avoided becoming an early source of

FIGURE 1 *Mary Pickford*

the scandal discourse. Instead of scandal, 'the Pickford-Fairbanks affair was recuperated in a family discourse', with the two stars 'touted as the country's ideal couple' (1990: 123).

Pickford fought to achieve independence in her dealings with the studios, making her most direct gesture in 1919 when, following rumours the studios were intending to cap star salaries, she and Fairbanks joined with Griffith and Charlie Chaplin (the most highly priced male star of the period) to form United Artists (UA). United Artists functioned as a distribution company for the films produced by the star names, placing the owners in a position where they could extend their economic power by negotiating more broadly across the film industry. Tino Balio explains:

> As heads of their own production companies, [the stars] controlled all artistic aspects of their work – from the creation of the scenario, to the selection of the director, to the final cut. By organising a distribution company, they could oversee, in addition, the crucial function of sales, advertising, and publicity. (1987: 10)

This power was evident with Pickford's first UA release, Paul Powell's *Pollyanna* (1919) in which she reprised her little girl image in the title role. *Pollyanna* was produced through Pickford's own company and distributed by UA. Whereas the established business practice in the exhibition sector was to lease prints from distributors for a fixed fee, *Pollyanna* was made available only on the basis of both a guaranteed base rental fee together with a percentage split of box office income. Despite complaints, exhibitors agreed to UA's terms, transforming the business model for dealings between distributors and exhibitors.

During the 1920s, Pickford's career would experience rises and falls in the star's critical and financial status. Despite taking more adult roles, the movie-going public were reluctant to let Pickford shed her child-woman image. From its inception, United Artists experienced decades of financial crises, the cause of which has been partly attributed to the company's star management. When Pickford eventually sold her UA stock in 1951 to Arthur

B. Krim and Robert S. Benjamin, partners in the law firm Phillips, Nizer, Benjamin and Krim, she described UA as 'sick unto death' (quoted in Balio 1976: 9). At the height of her appeal however, Pickford had clearly demonstrated the wide ranging power that the star could wield across all sectors of the film industry. Pickford's significance is not limited to the silent era. She exemplified many of the trends that would develop the Hollywood star system in future decades. In particular, Pickford showed how the star could have the ability to use his or her popular status as leverage to demand from producers rapid rises in salary payments. Her career also paved the way for stars to participate in box office earnings from the films they appeared in and represented the benefits to be had from stars choosing to form their own independent production companies. These trends would all become key characteristics of the star system following the decline of the vertically integrated studio system that dominated Hollywood in the 1930s and 1940s (see the following chapter). Pickford was therefore not only a product of the star system in the cinema. She showed how it was possible for stars to find ways to work that system for their own gain.

The Foundations of Hollywood Stardom

The star system in American cinema developed through the detailed division of labour, the redefinition of performance space in narrative film, and the widespread distribution of knowledge about individual film performers. Tracing the emergence between 1907–1922 of different types of discourse about film performers, Richard de Cordova not only provides an early history of the star system in American cinema but also identifies levels of knowledge relevant to reading and understanding star images at all stages of cinema history. While the discourse on acting reveals the general labour of film performance, the naming of picture personalities makes known individual performers through their on-screen professional existence. Naming enables the construction of the personality's image and identity across films, but also in other media such as newspapers and magazines.

De Cordova reserves star discourse to describe the extension of knowledge about film performers beyond on-screen appearances and into the off-screen lives of performers. With the star scandal, a star's private life becomes further divided between a publicly controlled private-image and a hidden secret private-image. From de Cordova's study, a general definition emerges of the star 'as actor (professional manipulator of signs), as picture personality (as a personality extrapolated from films), and as a star (as someone with a private life distinct from screen image)' (1990: 146–7). Although the discourses of actor, personality and star become levels of knowledge, with each seeming to add a further degree of depth to a star's image, these levels do not operate separately but work together as what de Cordova calls 'collapsing levels of identity' (p. 111).

As the example of Pickford shows, the Hollywood industry and the stars themselves were quick to exploit the value of star identity as a personal monopoly. Naming is essential to making that identity into a commercial and legal entity and the star system would develop through the use of such mechanisms to construct star identities and to use those identities as a means of promotion in the public domain. Subsequent phases in the development of the system would therefore be marked by transitions in the film industry as a whole which influenced this control and use of star identities.

3   CONTROLLING THE SYSTEM

With the star system in place, Hollywood worked hard to find effective means to exploit the identities of popular performers. By the end of the 1920s, economic control of the American film industry was concentrated in the hands of five leading companies: Paramount, Warner Bros., the Fox Film Corporation (Twentieth Century Fox after 1935), Radio Keith-Orpheum (RKO), and MGM, the film production studio of the exhibition conglomerate Loew's Inc. In this period, the star system operated under the general direction of these studios. The studio era of the 1930s and 1940s was a period in which Hollywood worked actively to make and market its stars. Stars became a vital asset in maintaining the hegemony of the major studios over the whole domestic film industry, with the effect that control of the film market required the strong control of its stars. This chapter will look at the structural conditions that enabled the Hollywood studios to dominate the film market in the United States and the ways in which those studios created, sold and controlled their stars.

American Cinema in the 1930s and 1940s

The power of the 'Big Five' studios, as they became known, was based on maintaining subsidiaries that engaged in the production, distribution and exhibition of films. With interests in all sectors of the film business, the major studios formed vertically integrated corporations, capable of recognising profits from all stages of the value chain by owning the means to make, sell and show films. Three other studios held a significant presence in the industry: Universal and Columbia functioned as producers and distributors, and United Artists distributed the films of major independent producers. Without their own exhibition outlets, the 'Little Three' released their films through the theatre chains run by the majors.

Although the studios have historically remained famous for the films they made, it was the control of exhibition rather than production that accounted for the power of the studios. The major studios controlled the domestic film market in the United States through their ownership of first-run theatre houses. For example, Paramount evolved from the theatre business started by Adolph Zukor, and became the largest of the vertically integrated companies after merger with the theatre operator Publix in 1925. Of the assets owned by the majors, investment was divided approximately into five per cent production and one per cent distribution, with exhibition accounting for the remaining ninety-four per cent. As Douglas Gomery argues, to gain 'a clear picture of the studio era one has to characterise the Big Five as diversified theatre chains, producing features, shorts, cartoons, and newsreels to fill their houses' (1986: 8).

While the power of the majors lay in their control of exhibition, in the domestic market the majority of theatres were owned by large or small independent exhibitors. The collective theatre holdings of the Big Five accounted for only twenty-five per cent of the total theatres in the United States. Ownership of theatres by the majors was, however, strategically planned to maximise earnings from admissions. The situation varied between different areas and locations. In some locations, the majors dominated the local market by acquiring or building the main first-run houses. Elsewhere, particularly in the largest cities of the United States, neighbourhood or subsequent-run theatres were more important. Theatre building and buying therefore followed local patterns of movie-going (see Huettig 1944).

Although the majors were in principle competitors, they nevertheless colluded in mutually beneficial ways. To meet the demand for new product in their own theatres, the majors would book films from other members of the Big Five and the Little Three. Also, the geographical siting of theatres in the domestic market was divided up so as to prevent the major exhibitors encroaching on territory controlled by other vertically integrated studios. Paramount dominated the South, New England, and the upper Midwest, with Fox taking the Far West, Warners controlling the mid-Atlantic states, and Loew's and RKO dividing New York, New Jersey and Ohio between them (see Gomery 1986). The first-run theatres of the majors therefore represented only a fraction of the total theatres in the country, however ownership was strategically organised to control the entire domestic market.

Alongside the theatres they directly owned, the majors also organised deals with independent theatres. Outside of the films produced by majors, it would be impossible for independent exhibitors to find any suppliers with a sufficient volume of films to fill their screens all year round. Although small independent producers did exist, independent exhibitors were reliant on the majors for supplying the bulk of the films shown. This situation placed the majors in a position to force non-competitive trading practices in their dealings with independent exhibitors. Block-booking involved distributors selling films as a package rather than individually and any block of films would combine major quality releases with more average and poor product. A price was set for the whole package, offering top titles at a lower price than they could be bought individually, while effectively raising the price of poor films. For the major distributors, block-booking had the advantages of guaranteeing sales of films in volume and spreading marketing costs across a whole group of films rather than individual titles. Blind-selling was a related practice, through which films were sold to exhibitors with maybe only a catalogue description or number as a reference. The status and profitability of the first-run theatres owned by the majors was protected by the further trade practices of clearance (determining the number of days to pass between runs in theatres) and zoning (setting regional areas in which clearance conditions applied). Large independent chains were able to use their size to negotiate the terms set by the majors but smaller independent exhibitors were compelled to accept such terms.

The most important effect of block-booking was the closing of the market to independent producers. For any exhibitor, the amount of playing time available in any week or year was limited. The first-run market, in which the highest revenues could be earned, was dominated by the chains owned by the majors. Through block-booking, independent exhibitors were compelled to buy films in such volume that their screens would be filled all year round with the supply of films from the majors. As the small independent exhibitors were dependent on continuing their relations with the majors for supplying both the quality and quantity of titles needed to fill theatres, there was little or no space in the market for independent producers. Control of exhibition therefore enabled the majors to collude to the mutual benefit of each other, while also preventing the growth of competition. By concentrating control of the market in the hands of so few companies, the studio system of the 1930s and 1940s formed a powerful oligopoly (see Balio 1985b).

Stars and Studios

Domination of the domestic film market by the major studios determined the conditions under which all categories of film performers could work in Hollywood during the 1930s and 1940s. The majors instituted mechanisms designed to produce and reproduce the star phenomenon by actively working to manufacture and take legal control of star identities. To retain control of their talent, the studios employed stars on contracts which could run for a maximum of seven years, and which were frequently written in terms that allowed the studios to manage and effectively exploit the images of stars. With the studios controlling exhibition, even star performers would find that it was virtually impossible to work outside the studio system. However, while the stars needed the studios, the studios also needed the stars. The power of star image was recognised not only by the studios but also by the stars themselves, and the period experienced significant instances of struggles between stars and the studios.

At the height of their power, the studios would keep many stars under contract, providing a 'stable' of performers from which to draw when making casting decisions across the studio's output. In order to achieve variety and feed the uncertainties of changing audience tastes, all the major studios established their own departments for discovering and developing new talent. Through his interviews with former studio employees, Ronald Davis (1993) uncovers the common processes that hopeful performers would have to pass through before they would be signed by a studio. Each studio employed their own talent scouts, for example Solly Baiano at Warner Bros., Lucille Ryman and Al Trescony at MGM, Milton Lewis at Paramount, and Ivan Kahn at Twentieth Century Fox. Scouts attended the theatres and night-clubs of New York and Los Angeles in the search for potential new stars. Other talent would come from vaudeville, burlesque and radio.

Scouts filed reports on interesting performers, which were circulated to studio executives, producers and directors. Those performers who caught the eye would be asked to read a scene for the scout who may then recommend that the performer attend the studio for tests. In tests, the try-out performers would prepare a suitable scene selected by the studio's drama coach. Usually hopefuls would have a silent test, shot in black and white in a studio, followed by a sound test. Based on these tests, the casting director would decide who would receive a contract, with the final approval resting with the studio head. Contracts offered starting salaries of between $75 and $250 a week, with a six-month option that allowed the studio to drop a performer after that period or raise his or her salary. Once signed to the studio, new talent would undergo an apprenticeship, during which time the studio would begin to mould the images of contract players. Apprentices would receive tuition from the studio's own speech and diction coaches, together with acting classes with the drama coach and, in some cases, singing and dancing lessons. Other optional lessons were offered in etiquette, movement, fencing, horseback riding, swimming, boxing and languages. Advice on fashion, make-up, and skin care were also available.

The earliest years of the film star system had put a high premium on the circulation and signification of a performer's name. Where an apprentice performer's actual name was regarded as inappropriate for his or her image, the studios made changes. Through make-up and hairstyling, alterations were also made to physical appearances. When their preparation was complete, newcomers would serve an apprenticeship by taking supporting roles chosen by the casting director. It would be usual to first try new talent in B-pictures. Frequently the placing of a new contract player would alternate a starring role in a B-feature, with a role opposite an established star in a major feature. Young performers of similar status might be paired in productions designed to test the partnership.

While stars could be profitable for the studios, they were also costly. From the earliest years of the star system, producers expressed concern that popular box office performance would lead to the escalation of performer earnings. Stars of the silent era, like Mary Pickford and Charlie Chaplin, had set the trend for stars to demand dramatic rises in their earnings. In the studio system, stars received salaries at levels that confirmed the biggest names as Hollywood's aristocracy. In research for his study of the 'movie colony', Leo Rosten (1941) found that in 1939, of respondents who had obtained some form of work acting in the movies, nearly eighty per cent earned under $1,000 a week, with six per cent receiving over $2,000 a week. In the same year, figures showed around sixty-nine per cent of actors earning less that $10,000 for the year, with four per cent enjoying salaries in excess of $100,000 a year. For many leading stars, income levels easily topped those of the highest paid studio executives.

During the early 1930s, the studios witnessed a wave of unionisation by labour groups organising to achieve representation and recognition for collective bargaining over pay and conditions. Compared to the skilled crafts, creative talent organised relatively late. Actors Equity was established in 1913 as the representative of stage actors. After winning recognition from Broadway producers in 1919, for several years Equity tried unsuccessfully to unionise film performers. In 1927, the formation of the Academy of Motion Picture Arts and Sciences was created as a professional body to represent five categories of creative labour: producers, directors, writers, technicians, and actors. Membership of the Academy was not open but restricted by invitation to those figures, including stars, believed to have made a significant contribution to the industry. Several functions were performed by the Academy, including its role as a collective negotiating agency in the conciliation and arbitration of labour disputes (see Clark 1995). As a producer-backed and controlled body, however, the Academy operated as a company union, proving to be ineffectual when representing the interests of its members in disputes with the studios.

The representation of screen actors by the Academy was tested twice during 1933. First, using the crisis conditions of the Depression as a convenient excuse for salary cuts, the studios introduced an eight-week salary waiver for employees. While raising objections to an all-out withdrawal of salaries, the Academy provided the studios with an income-linked formula for proportionally cutting salaries. Employees on the lowest rates of pay lost nothing, but others forfeited anything from twenty-five per cent of salary, while the highest paid, including stars, lost half their income (see Ross 1941). Secondly, when President Roosevelt passed the National Industrial Recovery Act (NIRA) in June, requesting all industries to draw up codes for stabilising the economy, studio executives and producers took the opportunity to draft articles intended to increase their control over stars. Articles were presented which intended to contain the salary demands of stars by prohibiting star-raiding between studios and preventing competitive bidding for stars. The code also sought to bring agents under the control of studio management, directly threatening the status of agents as independent mediators between talent and studio management. In response, the Academy adopted a moderate position by only asking for modifications to the articles rather than their wholesale rejection.

While these articles were later withdrawn, the disputes that ensued around the studio code exposed the Academy as a producer-controlled company union, unable to fight for the interests of screen actors. Consequently, in June 1933, performers independently organised by forming the Screen Actors Guild (SAG). While SAG became an agency of organised labour, David Prindle (1988) notes that choosing the identity of a guild, rather than a union, placed SAG in a non-militant relationship with studio management. Prindle argues that the social and political conservatism of many SAG members immediately avoided the militancy of organised labour, with the title 'Guild' suggesting instead a 'medieval association of artisans' (1988: 22). Another distinctive feature of SAG was that the body was established as a corporation. Prindle regards this as a move designed to attract stars to the organisation by insulating members from the financial responsibility they would otherwise incur for collective action.

In the years after its formation, SAG would engage in disputes with studio management, frequently uniting in support of other labour groups. However, the political credentials of SAG were clear, for these disagreements were usually settled at the expense of those other labour organisations. For example, in April 1937, SAG offered its support to the more leftist Federation of Motion Picture Crafts (FMPC), who were striking over the issue of recognition. When SAG leaked rumours of supporting strike action, senior figures in the guild met privately with Louis B. Mayer of MGM to demand studio recognition of SAG as the official bargaining agency for screen actors. After Mayer agreed on behalf of the studios to the guild's demands, SAG immediately withdrew support for the strike, a betrayal that eventually saw the collapse of the FMPC.

It is debatable to what extent stars can play an active role in organised labour. While stars could raise the profile of SAG both inside and outside the industry, they were also the quintessential embodiment of sheer individualism and therefore appeared to occupy a difficult position in relation to collective action. SAG represented all screen actors and included star names amongst its members. Eddie Cantor, the popular radio and film comedian, became the second president of SAG in 1933, and Fredric March, Adolphe Menjou and Robert Montgomery were elected vice-presidents. Star power could be effective. For example, Cantor used his personal friendship with President Roosevelt to have removed those clauses in the draft NIRA code that were of concern to the guild.

Stars were, however, also the elite of the performer labour pool, and as such enjoyed privileges that were not granted to other actors. The membership of SAG straddled the broad range of labour power differences amongst the community of film actors. Stars would have a stake in the collective agreements reached between SAG and studio management, however it was the case that stars had most to gain from individually negotiating over the uses of their labour and images. Like all agencies of organised labour, SAG was formed to negotiate the terms of collective bargaining. With stars, negotiations were not based on the collective terms and conditions but the particular uses of the star's personal monopoly. Frequently, the highly restrictive terms offered by the studios in the contracts of stars became a matter of heated dispute, and several stars would engage in personal battles with the studios. These individual instances of opposition are returned to later in this chapter.

Case Study: MGM – 'more Stars than there are in Heaven'

Metro-Goldwyn-Mayer (MGM) remained at the forefront of the studio system throughout the 1930s and into the early 1940s. During the 1930s, MGM's profits consistently exceeded those of any other studio, and only dropped behind Paramount and Twentieth Century Fox during the Second World War. MGM stood for Hollywood glamour in the studio era, boasting the claim that the studio employed under contract 'more stars than there are in heaven'.

   Although identified as a studio in its own right, MGM was actually the film production and distribution company of a larger entertainment conglomerate, Loew's Inc. Marcus Loew founded his People's Vaudeville Company in 1904, running cheap 'nickel vaudeville' with shows combining live variety entertainment and film shows (see Gomery 1986). Building a lucrative chain of theatres, Loew aimed to feed his screens with in-house productions, buying the film production and distribution company Metro Pictures in 1920, followed in 1924 by acquisition of the struggling Goldwyn Pictures. Ex-Metro executive Louis B. Mayer was appointed to oversee production and Metro-Goldwyn-Mayer was formed. A key figure at MGM was the young producer Irving Thalberg. Before illness in 1932, Thalberg oversaw all productions at MGM, and his role exemplified what Janet

Staiger (1985b) calls the central producer system of production. When Mayer down-graded Thalberg's responsibilities by reorganising the studio around the producer-unit system of production, the producer still packaged some of the most star-studded projects produced by MGM before his death in 1936.

Although Loew's business was founded on ownership of theatres, the number of cinema houses owned by the company was substantially lower than the other major studios. For this reason, MGM's success was always highly dependent on sales of its releases to the theatres of the other studios and independents. Douglas Gomery (1986) views this condition as requiring MGM to consistently produce high profile, popular releases. This imperative resulted in films with spectacular, glossy production values but also, Gomery argues, the largest stable of glamorous stars contracted to any studio.

MGM's glamour was well represented by Greta Garbo, Joan Crawford, Norma Shearer and Clark Gable. Mayer signed Garbo when she left Sweden and made her Hollywood debut in *The Torrent* (1926) before reaching prominence opposite John Gilbert in *Flesh and the Devil* (1926). Garbo's image was founded on romantic mystique, a quality which, in the context of Hollywood, was bound up with her sense of European otherness. MGM exploited that mystique to good effect. Moving into the sound era, MGM created an event around the marketing of *Anna Christie* (1930) with the advertising line 'Garbo Talks!' offering the teasing prospect of hearing the Scandinavian star speak. As her box-office power began to wane in the late 1930s, MGM broke the icy cool image by casting Garbo in the extremely successful comedy *Ninotchka* (1939), acknowledging the casting against type by advertising 'Garbo Laughs!'.

Although stars like Garbo and Gable brought charm and sex appeal to the studio, MGM's star stable was not all glamour. During the early 1930s, the studio's most popular star was Marie Dressler, who was already fifty-eight at the time she first worked for MGM in 1927. Working in the historical context of the Depression years, Dressler's popularity may be explained by the type of hard-working and resilient characters she portrayed. If Garbo and Gable represented the glamorous star, Dressler could be described as a 'down-to-earth star' (Balio 1995: 146), a category which saw her well matched with the equally down-to-earth Wallace Beery. Dressler and Beery were cast opposite each other in *Min and Bill* (1930) and *Tugboat Annie* (1933). Beery had a varied background in entertainment, working in circus, variety and Broadway theatre before entering films. After moving from Paramount to join MGM, Beery appeared to critical acclaim in *The Big House* (1930) and *The Champ* (1931), and gave a memorable performance as Long John Silver in *Treasure Island* (1934).

The MGM stable also nurtured a number of child and teenage stars, including Freddie Bartholomew, Jackie Cooper, Deanna Durbin and Judy Garland. Mickey Rooney was not only the most popular of this collection of young actors, but during the 1930s he also occupied the top slot in the star rankings three years in a row. After appearing as the character Mickey McGuire in a series of silent comedies between 1927 and 1933, Rooney signed to MGM in 1934. He played the central character in the Andy Hardy series of fifteen features, including *A Family Affair* (1937). In the late 1930s, Rooney began his partnership with Garland, MGM's other leading young performer, and the two were teamed across several movies, including *Thoroughbreds Don't Cry* (1937), *Love Finds Andy Hardy* (1938), *Babes in Arms* (1939), *Strike Up the Band* (1940), *Babes on Broadway* (1941) and *Girl Crazy* (1943).

Thalberg frequently brought together MGM's star stable in showcase productions. Based on Vicki Baum's best-selling novel 'Menschen im Hotel', *Grand Hotel* (1932) offered the paradoxical construction of a star-driven ensemble, with a cast that featured Garbo, Crawford, Beery and brothers John and Lionel Barrymore. Thalberg united the Barrymore brothers in *Arsène Lupin* (1932) and *Dinner at Eight* (1933) and created a showcase of Barrymore siblings when the brothers were cast opposite their sister Ethel in *Rasputin and the Empress* (1932). The star ensemble was most directly foregrounded in the short *Jackie Cooper's Christmas Party* (1932), in which young Jackie Cooper decides to throw a party and is helped out by his other friends at MGM – including Beery, Gable, Dressler, Shearer, and Lionel Barrymore, amongst others – who all appeared as themselves.

FIGURE 2 *Judy Garland*

MGM's stable of stars carried the studio through the 1930s. While other studios faced severe financial problems in the Depression years, MGM remained profitable. In the economic conditions of the 1930s, Loew's comparatively small chain of theatres was an advantage, demanding less investment and expenditure on general running costs than the larger chains. During the war and the immediate post-war years of the 1940s, however, the domestic film market enjoyed a boom period, and the size of Loew's chain prevented the company from adequately capitalising on this growth (see Gomery 1986). Consequently, MGM dropped behind the other majors, precipitating a downward spiral in fortunes which even the studio's star power could not reverse.

Selling Stars

Stars are crucial to the distribution of films. Distribution combines the functions of selling movies to exhibitors and marketing films to the general public. Starting with the circulation of the discourses of stardom before 1920, star identities not only became known but also marketable. During the 1930s and 1940s, the studios all maintained publicity departments with responsibility for constructing and disseminating a star's image across the media of posters, photographs, newspapers, magazines and radio. Publicity circulated a star's image both among fellow members of the industry and the general public.

At each studio, there would be a head or director of publicity responsible for managing the organisation of marketing campaigns. For example, MGM had Howard Strickling, while the same role was occupied by Harry Brand at Twentieth Century Fox, and Bob Taplinger at Warner Bros. At MGM the publicity department employed a large staff of approximately sixty, who individually took responsibility for three or four stars and liaison with a handful of national press correspondents (see Davis 1993). During the making of a film, the studio would assign a unit publicist to create and manage the publicity surrounding an individual production. Leading up to the release of a film, publicity departments would prepare stories from the set about the production and its stars, which were then positioned by 'planters' in trade and news media in ways intended to maximise exposure – publicity was not an afterthought in the production process. As one former publicist commented, 'publicity began when Warner Bros. bought a story; it never stopped until the picture was released' (quoted in Davis 1993: 142).

Aside from the in-house studio publicists, relatively unknown performers would hire an external publicity agent in the hope that such services may help the performer achieve star status (see Powdermaker 1951). Established names would also use publicity agents, either to cultivate competitive interest for the star's services inside the industry, or else to find ways beyond the studio publicity machine by which to manage the ways in which his or her image was directed at the public. In the latter case, however, hiring a publicity agent represented a bid by the star to exercise some degree of independent control over his or her image. Publicity agents were therefore not welcomed by the studios and stars were actively discouraged from hiring such mediators (see Gaines 1992).

To measure the value of stars, research companies were hired to conduct studies to assess the popularity of performers. Various methods of assessment were used to quantify popularity, including measuring the volume of fan mail received by a star, or analysing box-office statistics to assess a star's economic value. However, use of star ratings was seen to be a more scientific test of popularity. Ratings studies would look at the appeal of either a group of stars or conduct in-depth studies into an individual star's popularity. Star ratings were based on interviews with movie-goers, who were invited to indicate their response to the names of well-known performers (see Handel 1950). Ratings assessed a performer's popularity over a period of time and relative to that of other performers. Analysis would also be conducted into the effect of different types of films on a star's popularity, together with studies measuring popularity against audience demographic and social variables of sex, age, income and geography. Other studies would assess the 'want-to-see' factor, speculating on the popularity of a star's appearance in a forthcoming film.

In her study of Bette Davis's early career at Warner Bros., Cathy Klaprat examines how the star's image was reworked across publicity media and her narrative roles. Davis came to public prominence with her performance as Madge in *Cabin in the Cotton* (1932), a role Klaprat describes as a 'rich spoiled flirt' (1985: 356). Advertising for the film constructed the image of

Davis as a blonde sex bomb. The poster portrayed Davis and male star Richard Barthelmess in a kiss, eliciting audiences with the call 'Meet a new kind of temptress! Flaming as southern suns, bewitching as plantation moons, she'll teach you a new kind of love'. Klaprat suggests publicity worked on this occasion to depict Davis as a 'love expert' (p. 366). After her appearance in *Cabin in the Cotton*, the trade paper *Variety* ranked Davis as the top box-office attraction for 1932.

Building on her success, the following year Warner Bros. cast Davis again in the role of the sexy blonde. Publicity for *Ex-Lady* (1933) sold the new film through making direct reference to Davis's role in *Cabin in the Cotton* but when the film failed at the box office, Davis's name was not amongst the 1933 list of box-office leaders. Davis was loaned out to RKO for *Of Human Bondage* (1934), the film which Kalprat sees as redefining Davis's image around the role of the vamp. Davis's character, Mildred Rogers, destroys the gentle Philip Carey, played by Leslie Howard. Initially, publicity down-played Davis's presence in the film, with her name in small print below that of Howard. When the film performed well at the box office, Davis's name increased in size.

After her stint at RKO, Davis returned to Warner Bros. and the studio did not revert to the image of Davis as sexy flirt but instead capitalised on the image of the man-eating vamp she had so evocatively created while on loan. *Bordertown* (1935), starring Paul Muni, was included on the Warner production schedule in June 1934, but Davis was only cast as Marie Roark after *Of Human Bondage* proved successful. Publicity now linked Davis to her previous appearance as the vamp, and this image was replayed in her next role, appearing opposite Franchot Tone as Joyce Heath in *Dangerous* (1935). As Klaprat observes, the advertising for *Dangerous* foregrounded the vamp image, explicitly naming Davis in ways that linked her narrative role to the star's own identity. For example, posters announced 'Bette Davis smacks 'em where it hurts', 'Manwrecking Bette is on the manhunt again', and 'One look into Bette Davis' eyes and Tone joins Howard and Muni in succumbing to her fatal attraction' (Klaprat 1985: 368). Publicity therefore worked at constructing the vamp as a definition of Davis's fictional and real life identities.

To avoid the dangers of exhausting Davis's star value, Warner Bros. experimented with the mechanism of off-casting – giving the star roles that contradicted her vamp image. Klaprat sees Davis cast in a series of roles as 'the good woman', a type in which she appears as the saviour rather than destroyer of men. This new image first appeared with *That Certain Woman* (1937), after which Klaprat observes a pattern emerging as Davis's roles alternate between the good woman and the vamp. In *The Letter* (1940), Davis returned to the vamp, followed by the good woman in *All This and Heaven Too* (1940). This pattern continued with her vampish roles in *The Little Foxes* (1941) and *In This Our Life* (1942), and compassionate roles in *The Great Lie* (1941) and *Now Voyager* (1942). As Klaprat suggests, 'Offcasting not only provided the variation to sustain audience interest, but also served to enhance the image of the star as a great performer' (1985: 375). This diversity of roles itself became an image that could be publicised, with advertisements for *The Corn is Green* (1945) claiming 'There are as many Bette Davises as there are Bette Davis-starring pictures! That's part of Miss Davis's greatness: the ability to make each character she plays stand by itself, a distinct and memorable triumph of screen acting' (quoted in Klaprat 1985: 375).

Publicists would plant stories about stars in the trade and popular press but the primary publicity tool was the press book. Publicity departments would prepare a separate press book for each film released. Press books were mailed to exhibitors with the intention of offering theatres useful information and advice for publicising films. It was standard for the press book to include a cast list and synopsis of the film. The book would provide a display of advertisements and posters available to exhibitors for display in windows, theatre lobbies or the local press (see Sennett 1999). The publicity department would also send press books to newspapers, including prepared reviews for those local papers and radio stations that did not hire their own film critics. These various materials all found a point of focus and coherence in the images of stars. Press books included short biographies of the leading players in the films, accompanied by photographic portraits of stars. The graphic style of posters and advertisements would also foreground the role of stars. For

Dark Victory (1939), the Warner Bros. publicity department prepared reviews focusing on the performance of Bette Davis, along with printed quotes from the star and her character, and a range of posters portraying Davis. The images of stars were therefore central to publicity campaigns, and in the assortment of materials included in the press book, exhibitors were offered a pre-packaged version of a star's image available for local marketing drives.

Stars were also used in other methods of promotion, including personal appearances and road shows. Personal appearances would see stars turning up for glittery premieres in main cities. For the premiere of *Gone With the Wind* (1939), MGM not only transported the entire cast to Atlanta but also other stars contracted to the studio, including Claudette Colbert and Carole Lombard (see Sennett 1999). Personal appearances by musical stars were particularly effective, for a star could display his or her talents in song-and-dance numbers performed for the assembled public. For dramatic performers, the studio may have writers draft a special short scene for live performance, in which stars would play the roles in which they appeared in the film. Road shows required stars to make a succession of appearances on a tour of the cities and towns where a new release was opening. Bette Davis added to her reputation as a rebellious star when she flatly refused to participate in the ordeal and indignity of these tours (see Sennett 1999).

The marketing appeal of stars was not employed purely for the promotion of movies. Stars were also used to promote the sale of other products in secondary or ancillary markets. Charles Eckert (1978) sees the growth of a consumer economy in the United States during the 1920s as a period in which the film industry intensified efforts to link up with the high street in using star images to market household and fashion products. As suggested in the previous chapter, stars represent the ideological values of wealth, freedom and individualism on which a consumer economy is built. During the 1930s, stars were central to the development of Hollywood as a showcase for fashions, furnishings, accessories, cosmetics and other items available on the high street. An important development in the relationship between Hollywood and the high street came in 1930 when Bernard Waldman established the Modern Merchandizing Bureau. Waldman produced fashion lines based on clothing worn by female stars in films. All the studios (except Warner Bros., which launched its own Studio Styles in a similar capacity) provided Waldman with sketches or photographs of styles prior to the release of a film, and manufacturers would then produce styles based on these designs. The Bureau would send the completed garments to retailers, accompanied by publicity materials on the stars and the films. Initially, the studios offered styles for no charge, believing in the value of free advertising. Waldman opened his chain of Cinema Fashions shops and by 1937, the company owned 400 shops while also providing star-endorsed styles to nearly 1,400 other outlets.

With star-related promotions for cosmetics and toiletries, the Hollywood showcase addressed the market in ways that perceived women to be the primary category of consumer. Recognising the value of ancillary markets for the promotion of female stars, Hollywood cultivated the style of leading female stars such as Joan Crawford and Norma Shearer. It is important to also note the significance of this star glamour on the high street during the Depression years of the 1930s. Ready-to-wear lines offered the image of film star glamour but at relatively affordable prices. Star styles could thus promise some escape from real world conditions. Outside the United States, British women have recalled the enjoyment of sewing their own home-made copies of the styles worn by Hollywood's female stars during the Second World War, off-setting the hardship of wartime life (see Stacey 1994). Such actions are significant, for they indicate the pleasure of star identification, expressed in tangible forms produced outside of the consumer economy.

Case Study: Shirley Temple and the Business of Childhood

For four years between 1935 and 1938, Shirley Temple headed the list of top box-office stars in Hollywood. After successful starring roles in seven features during 1934, a special Academy award was bestowed on Temple – a miniature Oscar given in recognition of the child phenomenon.

Temple's success came from how she represented a concept of childhood that could appeal not only to children but adults as well. As Charles Eckert (1974) suggests, Temple's popularity was made through her appeal to universals: her cuteness, precocious talents and invocation of parental love. That vision of childhood was marketed not only through the star's films but also a huge merchandising industry that grew up around selling the Temple concept to Americans.

Temple's screen career started at Educational Films, a production company specialising in comedy shorts. In the early 1930s, Educational began production of the *Baby Burlesks*, a series of comedy shorts featuring child performers in satires of box-office hits from the time. Temple debuted for Educational in the unreleased *The Runt Page* (1932), a satire of *The Front Page* (1931), before appearing in *War Babies* (1932), a comedy take on *What Price Glory?* (1926). At the same time as working for Educational, Temple was loaned out to other studios, including supporting roles on *Red-Haired Alibi* (1932) for Tower Productions, *Out All Night* (1933) for Universal, *To the Last Man* (1933) at Paramount, and *As the Earth Turns* (1933) for Warner Bros.

Temple's work on features provided a stepping stone into the studio system. After an unaccredited appearance in *Carolina* (1934) for Fox Film, the studio conducted a number of 'try outs' to test her singing and dancing skills. Temple abilities were showcased in the revue film *Stand up and Cheer* (1934) after which, on 9 February 1934, she signed a seven-year contract with Fox. The following year, Fox merged with Twentieth Century Pictures, and Temple stayed with the studio until 1940. It was during her years at Fox that Temple would be transformed into a child star, yet it was on loan to Paramount when she received her first significant popular and critical acclaim with a role in *Little Miss Marker* (1934). When Paramount offered to buy out Temple's contract, offering her $1,000 a week against the $150 she was earning, Fox saw off the move to raid the studio's new talent. A revised contract was issued for $1,200 a week, rising by increments of $1,000 a week annually for seven years. The contract also included the conditions that Temple make only three films per year and her mother, Gertrude, be paid $150 a week to act as the child's coach (see

Edwards 1988). Shirley Temple's rapid rise to popularity meant that within a year Gertrude was able to re-negotiate a salary of $4,000 a week for her daughter and $500 for herself, with a $20,000 bonus for each film completed.

Temple's films dramatised both the anxieties and escapist fantasies of childhood. As Jeanine Basinger describes, the Shirley Temple film involved a familiar formula (1975: 11–13):

Shirley played an orphaned child adopted by a rich father ... or rich mother ... or perhaps a rich grandfather or grandmother. Or she played a child whose father wandered off absentmindedly, leaving her to cope. She was torn out of the arms of benefactor after benefactor ('Oh, please, Cap, don't let them take me away' ... 'I want my daddy' ... 'No, no, I don't want to go to any old orphanage'). This basic ingredient of the child alone was mixed together with crusts of old codgers, heaps of adoring adults, pinches of heartbreak, and generous helpings of poverty (which quickly melted into lavish living) – all stirred up with the subtlety of a McCormick reaper and garnished with a few songs and dances.

According to this narrative logic, the loss of one family is replaced by an idealised version of the family as an all-providing, all-caring unit. Through this drama of the family, Temple was able to appeal to both child and adult audiences. Basinger argues that adult audiences were drawn to Temple through the fantasy of childish escape she represented: 'The adult's fantasy was not so much to have a little girl like her (although that might do), but actually *be* her. To be taken care of, fussed over, listened to' (1975: 14 (emphasis in original)).

Eckert (1974) situates Temple's popularity against the background of crisis during the Depression era, and explains the star's appeal through the capacity of her image to displace the economic realities of the period. During the early 1930s, Eckert discusses how government-appointed bodies mounted an ideological war against appeals for state welfare.

Instead of state-funded welfare relief, the President's Organisation on Unemployment Relief and the Committee on Mobilization of Relief Resources espoused the values of charity against welfare, the act of giving rather than taking. Although not a direct reflection of state policy, Eckert views Temple's image as having a relevance for the period through performing a similar work of ideological displacement. In her films, Shirley's characters were frequently seen to come from humble backgrounds, however the realities of those social and political conditions were effaced. Instead, Shirley was seen to put hardship behind her with an overflowing bounty of love. Shirley solved the problems of others by her pure and unselfish acts of giving. This ideology of charity leads Eckert to argue that 'since her love was indiscriminate, extending to pinched misers or to common hobos, it was a social, even a political, force on a par with the idea of democracy or the Constitution' (1974: 68). Ideologically, therefore, the Temple image displaced the social and economic conditions of the era by offering a natural solution to the world's problems based on faith in the transformative power of love.

Such was the appeal of Temple's image that before the end of her first year at Fox, the studio was efficiently marketing the star in a range of secondary markets outside the film business, across a range of merchandise. In October 1934, *Playthings Magazine* carried the first advert for the Shirley Temple Doll from the Ideal Novelty and Toy Company (see Basinger 1975). A full wardrobe of clothes and other accessories was produced for the dolls. Sales of the dolls were so successful that in the first years of her career, Temple was earning more from the licensing of her image to Ideal than from her film work. Shirley Temple comics, colouring books and sheet music appeared, together with endorsed products such as soap, clothes, mugs, playhouses, and watches.

Although the narratives of Temple's films would achieve a sentimental resolution of childhood anxieties, Basinger regards Temple as offering a mixture of mischievous 'salty little wench' and 'out-and-out baby sexpot' (14). Both in her on- and off-screen lives, Temple displayed her gutsy handling of adult authority figures. On occasions, Temple appeared in roles as the 'little wife', tending the house for her father. The problematic sexual connotations of such a situation were barely masked, as Temple would sing to the father 'Marry me and let me be your wife', or 'In every dream I caress you'.

These sexual connotations of Temple's image were to blow up in public controversy. In his review of *Wee Willie Winkie* (1937) for the London magazine *Night and Day*, the British novelist Graham Greene (1937: 363) criticised the sensual display of the child star:

Wearing short kilts, she is a complete totsy. Watch her swaggering stride across the Indian barrack-square: hear the gasp of excited expectation from her antique audience when the sergeant's palm is raised: watch the way she measures a man with agile eyes, with dimpled depravity. Adult emotions of love and grief glissade across the mask of childhood, a childhood skin-deep.

Greene accused Temple of crudely appealing to an audience he characterised as middle-aged men and clergymen through her 'dubious coquetry' and 'well-shaped and desirable little body, packed with enormous vitality' (363). While the following libel case found against *Night and Day*, with the British judge calling Greene's review 'a gross outrage', the case exposed an underside to the Temple concept that was always at least implicit in her performances.

From the time she had first risen to stardom, observers had frequently speculated on how long Shirley Temple could retain her appeal as a child star. Falling box-office receipts led to her departure from Twentieth Century Fox in 1940 at the age of twelve. There followed a short period at MGM, in which her salary dropped dramatically from $9,000 to $2,500 a week (see Zierold 1965). MGM tried unsuccessfully to create projects teaming Temple with the studio's existing young stars, Mickey Rooney and Judy Garland. Completing only one film for MGM, Temple's teenage years were served on a seven-year contract (1943–1950) with Selznick International. David O. Selznick appeared uncommitted to reviving Temple's career and, during the period of her contract, she was loaned out to other studios, with her final feature coming with *A Kiss for Corliss*

(1949) for Strand Productions. Temple's association with childhood continued into adult years, appearing as the narrator of fairy tales in two television series: 'Shirley Temple's Storybook' (1958) for NBC and 'Shirley Temple Theater' (1960–1961) for ABC.

While Temple's fall from popularity was almost as swift as her rise to fame, her four-year domination of the star listings represented a more consistent record than most adult stars of the period. Through the Temple image, Fox was able to produce a clear and direct vision of childhood that could be marketed across films and in secondary markets during the 1930s. Although the child star may still appear an unusual and possibly eccentric phenomenon, Temple's stardom was not a peculiar aberration of the studio system, but rather the product of the studios' ability to construct star images that could make the most direct appeal to popular sensibilities and preoccupations.

Contracts and the Control of Star Image

In the 1930s and 1940s, stars were hired by the studios on contracts lasting for a maximum of seven years. During that period, the studio retained the exclusive option on the use of a performer's services. For performers new to the industry, a term contract with a studio offered an attractive and secure prospect. As a performer's career matured, however, the initial conditions laid out in the studios' contracts frequently proved restrictive. The term contract granted executives and producers an unprecedented level of control over the construction of a star's career and image. While contracts granted the studios the option to terminate a star's contract, the star had no legal right to break that contract (see Clark 1995). For the period of the contract, the studio had the power to determine a star's salary and control decisions over the productions and roles the performer would appear in. Contracts allowed for management to loan stars between studios and without the consent of the performer. In these arrangements, the renting studio would pay that star's salary plus an average of seventy-five per cent to the studio that held the star's contract (see Huettig 1944). The cost of hiring contracted stars from the studios was too high for most independent producers and the exchange of stars between the studios was one of the ways in which the majors collaborated to maintain their oligopoly.

Studio management held the contractual power to decide which and how many roles a star would play over a year, and control of casting allowed the studios to typecast stars (see Walker 1970). By offering a series of similar roles, the studio could unify the on-screen image of a star. Any star who showed dissent over the roles he or she was offered, or else refused to be loaned to another studio, faced the threat of suspension without pay. Following suspension, a star could expect to be offered less desirable roles at a lower salary. After the recalcitrant star returned to work, the contract allowed for the period of suspension to be added at the end of the original term, lengthening the total period for which a star was owned by the studio (see Gaines 1992). An alternative way of punishing a difficult star was to lend the performer to an independent production which was predicted to be unlikely to succeed at the box office. Mae Huettig described the latter option as 'the Hollywood equivalent of Siberia' (1944: 93).

Type casting created continuity across a star's on-screen image but contractual terms also extended to cover the private lives of stars in ways designed to protect against the possibilities of stars behaving in ways that threatened to bring any scandalous contradiction or discontinuity to the image. During the 1920s morality clauses were included as part of the standard personal services contract, with the effect that the private lives of stars also came under the scrutiny of the studios. As Jane Gaines suggests, the term contract offered the studios 'image insurance' (1992: 148). Stars therefore found that the term contract controlled both their on- and off-screen lives.

While the contracts of stars shared many common conditions, there was no uniform star contract. Individual terms could be negotiated by any star who could demonstrate his or her value to the studio. This was possible for stars who had achieved previous popularity in the theatre or at another studio. Stars who were a product of the studios' in-house talent development departments, however, faced greater difficulty negotiating better terms as they had signed their contracts before their rise to fame. Paul Muni was already well known as a stage star before he signed to Warner Bros. in the early 1930s. After making his screen debut for Howard Hughes in the independently produced *Scarface* (1932), Muni was signed by Jack Warner on a one-picture deal to appear in *I Am a Fugitive from a Chain Gang* (1932). When the film was a success, Warner offered Muni a two-year, eight-picture deal, with Muni receiving a salary of $50,000 per picture. Muni's deal granted many individual concessions: the approval of story, role and script; billing as sole star; loan outs to other studios contingent on the star's consent; a fifty-fifty split with Warner Bros. on any salary average paid by the borrowing studio; definition of a year as twenty-one weeks; and the right to take stage work between films (see Schatz 1988).

On occasions, stars did openly contest the restrictive conditions imposed by their contracts. Amongst the most famous contract battles between a star and a studio was the fight between Bette Davis and Warner Bros. In March 1936, when the studio refused to loan her to RKO for *Mary of Scotland* (1936), Davis delayed returning to the studio for additional work on *The Golden Arrow* (1936). Davis made a series of demands: a new contract for five years only; a salary rise from $100,000 to $200,000 per year; the limiting of her services to four pictures a year; star or co-star billing; and clauses granting her freedom to do one picture a year for another studio, her choice of cameraman and a three month holiday. When Jack Warner refused Davis's demands, she turned down the role offered to her in *God's Country and the Woman* (1937) and was suspended without pay. She promptly departed for England to make films for Toeplitz Productions.

Warner Bros. sued Davis for breach of contract, claiming that any film produced by the British company would compete with current releases from the studio. In an English court, Davis referred to the contract as a form of slavery. Warner Bros.' barrister Sir Patrick Hastings replied: 'This slavery has a silver lining, because the slave was ... well remunerated' (quoted in Warner Sperling *et al.* 1994: 220). In his summary for the defence, Davis's barrister Sir William Jowett argued 'Miss Davis is a chattel in the hands of the producer. I suggest that the real essence of slavery is no less slavery because the bars are guilded' (221). According to the negative service provision in Davis's contract, the British court found in favour of Warner Bros. and the star returned to the studio. The case showed that even a star of Davis's prominence could not escape the controlling power of the term contract. Davis stayed at Warners until 1948, completing *Beyond the Forest* (1949) before appearing in *All About Eve* (1950) for Twentieth Century Fox and *Payment on Demand* (1951) for RKO.

The practice of extending the contracts of suspended stars ended when Olivia de Havilland took Warner Bros. to court over the length of her contract. After refusing to work on *The Gay Sisters* (1942), *George Washington Slept Here* (1942) and *Saratoga Trunk* (1945), de Havilland's contract was due to expire with her performance in *Princess O'Rourke* (1943) and a loan to RKO for *Government Girl* (1944). When Warner Bros. claimed the contract had a further six months to serve due to periods of suspension, the studio added a third feature, intending to loan the star to Columbia. De Havilland took the studio to court, and in May 1944 the Supreme Court of California ruled she did not have to work the period added for suspension as this was a debt that violated the state's antipeonage laws (see Schatz 1998). De Havilland subsequently left Warner Bros. for Paramount. The victory affected not only de Havilland's career but also questioned the whole system of hiring stars on term contracts. Many stars would remain on term contracts into the 1950s, but the de Havilland incident was a landmark case that would lead to stars wresting control of their careers from the studios and seeking greater independence.

Case Study: Cagney vs. Warner Bros.

Davis and de Havilland were not the only stars to confront Warner Bros. over their contracts. James Cagney mounted a running battle with Jack Warner over many years during his time with the studio. Following a career in musical theatre, Cagney signed to Warner Bros. in 1930, appearing in a supporting role on *Sinners' Holiday* (1930). After working for William Wellman in a small role on *Other Men's Women* (1931), Cagney was cast by the director as second lead to Edward Wood in *Public Enemy* (1931). However, within days of starting rehearsals, the director had the actors exchange roles. Warner Bros. was the main producer of the gangster genre in the 1930s and in *Public Enemy* Cagney's portrayal of Tom Powers set an image that would stay with him throughout his years at the studio.

Versions of Cagney's gangster persona appeared most famously in *Angels With Dirty Faces* (1938) and *The Roaring Twenties* (1939). The popularity of Cagney's fighting gangster figure was a product of the Depression years and the immediate aftermath. Discussing the significance of the gangster hero in the context of the depression years, Nick Roddick suggests the gangster film 'showed characters responding actively and often with a strong sense of personal honour to social circumstances which, in real life, seemed to condemn their audiences to inactive frustration in the face of a "system" which often appeared *dis*honourable' (1983: 99, emphasis in original). Cagney never left behind his musical background and frequently appeared in comic roles, even playing Bottom in Max Reinhardt's production of *A Midsummer Night's Dream* (1935). It was most frequently the case, however, that Cagney would be cast as gangsters or, more generally, as figures outside the law.

In the 1930s, Cagney and studio head Jack Warner continually engaged in battles over the star's contract. Cagney expressed his dissatisfaction with the limited roles he was cast in and attempted to re-negotiate the terms of his contract with the studio. Following the release of the comedy *Blonde Crazy* (1931) Cagney took the occasion of the film's quick success to enter into his first conflict with Warner Bros.' management. Cagney complained that he was underpaid compared to other stars at Warner Bros. Jack Warner had succeeded in raiding Paramount's star stable by offering high salaries to Kay Francis and William Powell. Francis was paid $3,000 a week for forty weeks-a-year and Powell received $300,000 a year for two films (see Hagopian 1986). Joe E. Brown earned $5,000 a week and Douglas Fairbanks $1,750 a week. Edward G. Robinson, the

FIGURE 3 *James Cagney and Joan Leslie*

other major gangster star of the period, made $280,000 over eighteen months. Cagney demanded a rise in his salary from the standard $450 a week and, after several months of negotiations, at the end of 1931 signed a new contract for $1,400 weekly.

As Cagney became Warner Bros.' major box office attraction, the star continued to request that the studio raise his salary. While a rise in 1932 took Cagney to $3,000 a week for four films a year, the star continued to protest his terms of employment. Kevin Hagopian (1986) identifies several grounds for disagreement in Cagney's dealings with Warner Bros. Cagney was dissatisfied with the directors and leading ladies employed on his films. He also resented the studio's continued casting of him in variations on the gangster type. On more economic terms, Cagney believed the studio should offer him a share in the profits of films that performed well at the box office. While not a specific complaint against Warner Bros., Cagney also found that as his salary grew, so his tax burden increased, an issue that would become significant in the star's later career. Billing became an issue when the name of co-star Pat O'Brien appeared above Cagney's on the marquee for the release of *Devil Dogs of the Air* (1935). Cagney argued that the billing contravened the terms of his contract. As the case progressed through the courts, Cagney took a contract with the small and short-lived Grand National studio, making two films before Warner Bros. moved to settle out of court.

Cagney returned to Warner Bros. on favourable terms. According to the contract signed by Cagney in July 1939, the star was required to work a maximum of three films a year and to undertake a minimum of publicity work for the studio. The contract also gave him the option to reject a certain number of stories he was not suited to and the right to terminate his contract with five months notice. The contract gave Cagney $150,000 per picture plus ten per cent of the gross, and also required that William Cagney, the star's brother, be employed as associate producer on his films.

Although the new contract granted Cagney more control over his work, he left Warner Bros. after winning an Academy Award and second New York Critics prize for his famous performance as George M. Cohan in *Yankee Doodle Dandy* (1942). Cagney's departure was not brought on by any particular falling out with the studio but was the result of changing conditions in the industry during the early 1940s that favoured a move to independence. Potential gains for independent producers appeared imminent when, in 1940, the Justice Department began a series of actions, continuing through the decade, that ruled against the oligopolistic control of the studio system. Also, between 1940–1942, the Roosevelt administration pursued a policy of raising taxes to meet high levels of expenditure on defence, which would see the salary of high earners, including film stars, reduced to $25,000 net per annum. Independent production presented Cagney not only with control over his career but also with ways of securing income other than his salary, by means of investments and deferments. After leaving Warner Bros. Cagney signed for occasional films with Twentieth Century Fox before he and his brother formed Cagney Productions, Inc., signing an agreement in March 1942 which saw the company bankrolled as a production subsidiary of United Artists.

The management of Cagney Productions was mishandled. A record of financial extravagance and arguments over publicity resulted in an output of only three films in six years, and United Artists and Cagney Productions parted ways. With his previous history, it appears surprising that on 6 May 1949 Cagney signed a new contract with Warner Bros., taking Cagney Productions with him. *White Heat* (1949), Cagney's first film back at Warner Bros., returned him to the gangster type, however his power and status in the industry had changed. The new contract was non-exclusive and granted the star extensive decision-making powers together with a salary of $250,000 per picture.

Back in 1932, during one of his battles with Warner Bros., Cagney walked out on the production of *Blessed Event*. Returning to the studio, he was cast in a production that saw him take a typical role as a conman. Originally titled *Bad Boy*, the film was renamed *Hard to Handle* (1933), the irony of which was not lost on the studio's publicity machine. Advertising heralded 'the Movies' Prodigal Son-of-a-Gun Returns' and '... All is Forgiven' (quoted in McGilligan 1975: 45). During his time at Warners Bros. during the 1930s, the casting of Cagney as the tough and fast-dealing street hoodlum seriously limited his image. At the same time, however, that image also appeared to represent the star's combative and uncompromising attitude towards the studio system.

Stars as Property

In the 1930s and 1940s, the five vertically integrated Hollywood studios dominated the domestic film industry through their control of exhibition in the United States. By their strategic ownership of theatres across the country, the majors were able to maximise their profits while blocking the entry of independent producers into the business. Stars played a vital role in the studios' control of the American film industry. Established stars offered a means for attempting to stabilise audience demand, while inside the studios, departments also fed the star system through the organised development of new star identities. A variety of methods were used to construct and promote the images of stars and the effects of star appeal were felt not only in the film business but also in other areas of the consumer economy.

While powerful figures in the economics of the studio system, the professional freedom of stars was contained by contractual conditions under which they were employed by the studios. The term contract defined the relationship between the star and the studio in ways that served the economic interests of the studios first and foremost. For the duration of the contract, producers and studio executives were able to manipulate the career of the star. In certain cases, stars disputed their contractual obligations and actively resisted the use of their labour by studio management. Such was the extent of the studios' control over the domestic film market in the United States, however, that there existed no space in which to operate that was totally free of studio influence. In the studio era, stars found that they became the virtual property of the studios.

4   RETHINKING THE SYSTEM

From the late 1940s, conditions inside the film industry – and American society in general – led to the breakdown of the vertically integrated studio system. While the studios had built their power through domination of film exhibition, from the 1950s the studios began to see their role principally as distributors. The medium of television presented new opportunities for diversification into small-screen entertainment. Further change in the structure of the film industry occurred as, from the late 1960s, all the major studios were gradually acquired by larger corporations. This trend located ownership of the film business in a broader conglomerate structure and, with many of the new owners of the studios holding interests in other media industries, the Hollywood film business became positioned in a diversified entertainment marketplace. This chapter looks at the shaping of the star system in these contexts, initially examining the significant changes made to the business of stardom following the breakdown of the vertically integrated industry, followed by a look at stars in the age of conglomeration.

Hollywood Reorganisation

Inside the vertically integrated system of the studio era, the oligopolistic control of the domestic film business had caused independent exhibitors and producers to demand an end to the non-competitive practices that maintained the power of the studios. Although the Justice Department began antitrust proceedings against the majors in 1938, it was not until after the Second World War that these actions would impact on the industry. In December 1946, the decree was passed preventing studio distributors from continuing the practices of block-booking and clearances (see Conant 1981). Further change came in 1948, when the Supreme Court ruled that Paramount should divorce the company's theatre circuit from its production and distribution operations. The case affected the whole industry, with all the vertically integrated studios required to sign decrees consenting to divest their theatre holdings. Although all the studios eventually signed consent decrees, the industry did not change overnight, and Warner Bros., Twentieth Century Fox and MGM would not complete divestiture of their theatres until the 1950s.

At the same time as the studios were responding to the need for structural reform, the domestic audience for cinema in North America began to rapidly decline. Immediately after the Second World War, in 1946, the US box office achieved a historic high of 4,067.3 million admissions, an average of 78.2 million admissions each week. This high was achieved in an era when movie-going was a regular weekly ritual for Americans. By 1950, however, admissions had fallen to 3,017.5 million (58 million per week), and the figure continued to decline during the decade, with the 1959 box office recording 1,488.2 million (28.6 million weekly) admissions.

One important factor in the decline of the movie-going audience was the growth in popularity of television. In 1949, television ownership in American homes was estimated to stand at 940,000 sets. In 1950, four million sets were in use and by the end of the 1950s, ninety per cent of American homes were estimated to have television. However, television was not the only cause of the declining audience. As John Belton (1994) argues, during the 1950s the United States experienced other social changes that would have a significant impact on patterns of movie-going. A fall in the hours of the average working week, together with higher levels of disposable income, saw Americans preferring to spend their leisure time and money on participatory recreations such as gardening, golfing, hunting and fishing. Compared to cinema-going, television, with its in-home and constant on-demand entertainment, was more easily suited to fit these busy leisure lifestyles. A visit to the cinema therefore began to appear more of a special event than an established ritual. A further factor influencing patterns of cinema-going was the drive to suburbanisation. Post-war loans, cheap mortgages and the prosperous economy of the 1950s extended home ownership, resulting in a boom of house building in new out-of-town developments. As the suburbs began to characterise the ideals of domestic living for the period, these new residential spaces took audiences away from the urban centres where the main first-run theatre houses were located. In the 1950s, therefore, the film industry in America was forced to adapt to new structural conditions, together with a fall in the movie-going audience effected by the challenge of television and changing social conditions.

While the breakdown of the vertically integrated oligopoly may suggest the market was suddenly open to greater competition, history saw the studios continue to maintain their power. As the main suppliers of films to independent exhibitors and the circuits they had previously owned, the Hollywood studios transformed the nature of their power by re-orientating their business away from the control of exhibition and towards the control of distribution. While still making some of their own in-house productions, the studios increasingly acted as distributors for projects created by independent producers. When seen in this context, 'independent production' is a potentially misleading expression, for the financing of independent projects was frequently secured prior to production through the agreement of distribution deals with the studios. In their role as production financiers, the studios could still control competition from independent production, without facing the costs and risk of investing in an extensive in-house production slate.

With a declining audience, Hollywood cut back on the number of films produced each year. Previously, the films produced by the studios were guaranteed a market in the first-run houses and the studios had maintained factory-like production schedules to keep a constant flow of films into the theatres. This security was removed with the ending of block-booking and the divestiture of theatres, and the studios were now required to sell their films individually to theatres owned by separate corporations. This situation had a major effect on the organisation of production. To meet demand, production in the 1930s and 1940s was based on the central producer and producer-unit systems of production. As the demand for films decreased, Hollywood reorganised production around individual film projects. This change heralded the arrival of what Janet Staiger (1985c: 330) describes as the 'package-unit' system of production.

> Rather than an individual company containing the source of the labour and materials, the entire industry became the pool for these. A producer organised a film project: he or she secured financing and combined the necessary labourers ... and the means of production (the narrative 'property', the equipment, and the physical sites of production).

Staiger suggests that the impact of this change saw the end of the self-contained studio and the movement in the industry towards organising production around the film and not the firm. Rather than owning the entire means of production, which would be used across many productions, the unit making a film would lease or purchase resources for that project alone. The change to the package-unit system would dramatically effect the employment and status of stars in the industry.

Reworking the System

Package-unit production had several significant effects on the star system. With a lower volume of production, the studios sold off or leased their physical assets, and cut back on overheads by releasing staff from contracts. Stars, the most costly category of labour, were previously employed on term contracts extending up to seven years. With the move to package-unit production, stars became freelance labour, hired for short periods on separate film projects. In the new system of production, the packaging of a project involved the bringing together of key personnel during development. As Richard Dyer MacCann explains, a package 'usually consisted of a writer and his script, one or two stars, and even a director' (1962: 55). The creation of a package in the new freelance labour market gave increased powers to talent agents in the industry. Representing the services of their independent clients, agents began to replace the studio executives in the planning of productions. With stars hired on a film-by-film basis, stars and their agents were able to negotiate fresh terms for each project the star signed to. A successful box-office record could therefore enable star and agent to demand better terms with each new film project. For the most successful stars, it became possible to rapidly increase the fees for their services. Star wages therefore grew more rapidly than they had in the studio era, further extending the hierarchical division between stars and other film performers, and making the employment of stars an even more expensive cost in the budgeting of productions.

Block-booking had allowed films to be sold in such a way that poor products could be carried by high-profile features, with the costs of distribution and marketing spread across a body of films. As this practice was outlawed, and as Hollywood adapted to the package-unit system, films were sold individually, requiring a separate marketing campaign for every production. Each film now had to fare in the market according to its own merit. To differentiate a film in the new market, producers turned towards raising the production values of a film. The presence of high-profile stars acted as a simple and direct sign of production quality. When selling films on an individual basis, distributors turned to making the image of the star into the image of the film.

Under the regime of the studio term contract, stars were prevented from forming their own independent production companies. As stars were gradually released from the restrictions of the contract system, they explored the creative and economic advantages of running an independent. When Burt Lancaster signed a new contract with producer Hal Wallis in 1947, it was agreed the star would be allowed to accept outside work (see Fishgall 1995). At this time, Lancaster had formed a partnership with producer Harold Hecht, and together they launched Hecht-Lancaster Productions, making independent features, including *Apache* (1954) and *The Kentuckian* (1955). Following the conclusion of his contract with Wallis, Lancaster went fully independent in late 1956, joining with Hecht and associate Jim Hill to form Hecht-Hill-Lancaster, producing *Trapeze* (1956) and *Sweet Smell of Success* (1957) among other titles.

Other star-based independents formed at this time were Kirk Douglas's Bryna Productions, Tony Curtis and Janet Leigh's Curtleigh Productions, Jerry Lewis and Dean Martin's York Productions, and Marlon Brando's Pennebaker Productions. Creatively, the star-based independent companies allowed performers to take a broader role in decision making. Staiger (1985c) suggests that one of the effects of the package-unit system was that stars and other key talent such as directors became more involved in business dealings than matters of film-making. From an economic perspective, independent production also allowed high-earning stars to obtain tax advantages through listing income under capital gains rather than personal salaries (see MacCann 1962).

Initially seen as a threat to the film business, television was increasingly viewed as an area for growth by the studios. Looking for areas in which to diversify as the film market declined, the Hollywood studios became providers of programmes for television. After ABC launched Disney's weekly television show 'Disneyland' in 1954, other studios followed the drift towards programme production. In 1955, ABC ran 'Warner Bros. Presents' and 'MGM Parade', and 'The Twentieth Century Fox Hour' appeared on CBS (see Anderson 1994). Further ground for collaboration between the film business and television came from the sale of feature films to the networks. The small studios Monogram and Republic had quickly struck deals to sell their films to television, but the major studios at first refused. When RKO fell on hard times in the early 1950s, the former major was broken up and its assets were sold to the television industry. RKO's film library was sold in 1955 to a subsidiary of the General Tire and Rubber Company, General Teleradio Incorporated, which purchased the library of features for presentation on the six television stations they owned in major US cities (see Jewell and Harbin

1982). As the other studios also sold their pre-1948 libraries to the broadcasters, television became an accepted secondary market for feature films, thus becoming a new 'window' by which the film star system addressed the American public.

However, the new market for films also raised a fresh set of concerns over the legal control of star images. Two notable early disputes over the re-use of film performances featured the singing cowboy stars Gene Autry and Roy Rogers. Both Autry and Rogers had started careers as singers before starring as themselves in B-features for Republic Pictures during the 1930s. Alongside screen acting, both stars ran their own companies. Unlike the stars of the major studios, Rogers was able to develop his own separate company while under contract at Republic. The studio held the rights to Rogers's film work but the star's company held the right to exploit his image and that of his horse, Trigger (see Gaines 1992). Autry moved into television in 1950, starting his own company – Flying A Productions – to produce several series, including 'The Gene Autry Show' (1950–1956), 'Annie Oakley' (1954–1956) and 'The Adventures of Champion' (1955–1956).

In the early 1950s Rogers and Autry individually took Republic to court over the sale of their feature films for re-use in cut down form as television series episodes. Rogers complained that while Republic had the right to sell his films, television was an advertising-sponsored medium that located the use of his image in a context of commercial exploitation that his company had the right to control. Autry argued a different line, stating that cutting his films for television could detrimentally tamper with his image. In both cases, the courts ultimately ruled against the stars.

When RKO and the small studios had sold their films to the networks, they agreed residual payments would be made to actors for re-use of their performances. Other studios, however, refused such payments. For the Screen Actors Guild, the subject of residuals became a new area of concern in the television era. By 1960 the issue was not resolved and, in combination with demands over health, pension and welfare plans, in March of that year the guild called a strike. The studios held performance rights on all pre-1948 films but SAG was demanding that members be compensated for films after that time. David Prindle sees anti-strike reporting of the time arguing that actors wanted 'to be paid twice for doing one job', representing stars as the privileged elite of a 'country-club union' (1988: 85). Prindle also suggests that with many stars acting as independent producers, they experienced a conflict of interest during the strike. When support for the strike therefore inevitably wavered, SAG compromised, dropping demands for residuals on films between 1948–1960 when producers agreed to pay residuals beginning from 1960. Prindle suggests this outcome remains an embarrassing episode in the history of the guild, evoking bitterness amongst stars who see their pre-1960 work re-screened on television without remuneration to the performer. As the SAG agreements and the cases of Rogers and Autry indicate, television became a new battleground over the ownership and control of star images.

Case Study: MCA – the 'star-spangled Octopus'

During the late 1940s and 1950s, as the studio system was gradually dismantled, the most powerful agency in Hollywood was Music Corporation of America (MCA). As the studios reorganised, MCA's star client list enabled the agency to act responsively to the changing shape of Hollywood and negotiate a powerful position in the industry. Founded in 1924 by Dr Jules Stein, MCA served as a booking agent for dance bands in the Chicago area. After moving MCA to Hollywood in 1936, Stein hired the young Lew Wasserman as an agent. Wasserman quickly established his skill in brokering powerful deals for MCA film and music clients. In 1946, Wasserman became president of the Corporation, guiding MCA through the years of upheaval in Hollywood.

MCA's power was built on the impressive list of major stars it represented. In 1959 that list included the following: Carroll Baker, Leslie Caron, Charles Bickford, Ernest Borgnine, Marlon Brando, Montgomery Clift, Joan Collins, Joseph Cotton, Joan Crawford, Tony Curtis, Dorothy Dandridge, Joan Fontaine, Clark Gable, Van Heflin, Charlton Heston, William Holden, Howard Keel, Boris Karloff, Charles Laughton, Jack

Lemmon, Dean Martin, Marilyn Monroe, Gregory Peck, Anthony Perkins, Jane Russell, Joanne Woodward and Jane Wyman (see Canby 1959). MCA packaged film projects that brought together the agency's talent. *The Young Lions* (1958) was developed as a project to bring together leading MCA clients, Brando, Clift and Martin. For *Some Like It Hot* (1959), MCA packaged the director Billy Wilder with the film's stars, Curtis, Lemmon, and Monroe. Monroe's final film, *The Misfits* (1961), was another MCA package, casting her alongside fellow clients Clift and Gable.

Backed by the agency's entire star roster, MCA was able to aggressively pursue beneficial deals for individual clients. In 1950 Wasserman used the influence of MCA to broker a key deal between Universal and his client, James Stewart, for the star's work on *Winchester '73* (1950). The deal granted the star a participating share in profits from the film. Profit participation went back to the days when Mary Pickford had personally earned half the gross box-office receipts from her films. Similar terms were agreed in the 1930s by Mae West and the Marx Brothers.

When Stewart signed to *Winchester '73*, his star appeal was low, yet Wasserman's skill in deal making drove negotiations in the star's favour. Wassermann had Universal agree to sign Stewart on a deal that gave the studio rights to the Broadway stage success, 'Harvey', in which Stewart was appearing at the time, providing the studio agreed to the star also appearing in *Winchester '73*. For the film *Harvey*, Stewart would be paid $200,000 plus a share of net profits (i.e. profits after studio deductions for production and distribution costs), while for the second film the star would waive his salary in return for a fifty per cent share of gross profits (i.e. box office earnings before deductions) (see MacDougall 1998). With the first film predicted to be a sure fire hit and the second seen as a standard genre picture, Universal's William Goetz accepted Wasserman's terms. Universal also agreed to Wasserman's demands that Stewart be given sole star billing, along with approval of director and co-stars.

The deal had advantages for both star and studio. For the star, depending on the film's performance at the box office, the deal could potentially raise his cumulative earning power. For the studio, the deal allowed Universal to employ a major star name without paying up-front –

or at all if the film failed at the box office. When, contrary to predictions, the fortunes of the two films were reversed, Stewart made over $600,000. Stewart's was not the first profit participation deal but it became, for the time, the most profitable one. The deal made the issue of participations and the rights of approval key areas of negotiation in the new market of star labour.

MCA had started in the music industry before moving into film, and the agency's talent list provided a base from which to further diversify into television. With television growing as a popular medium in the United States, in 1952 MCA set up various subsidiaries, producing original television drama through Revue Productions, packaging live television shows as Management Corporation of America, and operating a television distribution arm, MCA-TV (see Canby 1959). Fearing that agents would be given too much power if they acted as both talent representatives and producers, in 1939 the Screen Actors Guild (SAG) had passed a regulation preventing agents from producing films. The reason for this fear was that if agents functioned as both the representative and management of labour, a conflict of interests would ensue between the producer's need to keep costs down and the requirement that an agency act in the most beneficial ways for clients. However, MCA's power was evident in July 1952, when SAG granted a blanket waiver allowing Revue to operate as a leading production outfit. Historians have questioned the role that Ronald Reagan, president of SAG and an MCA client, may have had in manipulating these negotiations (see Prindle 1988). What is certain, however, is that Reagan went on to work in Revue's 'GE Theater' anthology, starting on a salary of $125,000 and staying with the series for nine years.

During the late 1950s, MCA extended its presence in the film and television industries. In 1958, MCA paid $35 million for Paramount's library of pre-1948 films, and between 1959–62 MCA acquired Decca Records in a deal giving the agency control of Universal Pictures, previously acquired by Decca in 1952. As MCA extended its influence from leading star agency to multimedia conglomerate, the agency was nicknamed the 'star-spangled octopus'. This power had it limits, however, for the US Justice Department ordered MCA to divest the agency operations from its production interests and, in 1962, MCA left the agency business.

Although MCA ceased to be an agency, it nevertheless took an active role in starting several of the trends that redefined the star system following the reorganisation of the studios. MCA had played the role of packager, using its impressive list of stars to develop productions. Deals like that struck for James Stewart had exploited new possibilities in the earning power of stars in the freelance labour market. It was MCA which also saw the potential that the new popularity of television offered as a window for star talent. MCA may have moved on from its role as talent representative when diversifying into television production, but it was the power of stars which had made the company. Through its background in the successful management of star talent, MCA was able to respond to the changing conditions of Hollywood and to come to sit alongside the leading studios as a major provider of film and television entertainment.

Conglomeration and Diversification in the Entertainment Business

Following structural reorganisation during the 1950s, in the late 1960s Hollywood would experience a further period of major transformation, as ownership of the industry's main production/distribution companies changed hands. With cinema audiences continuing to decline from the 1950s, the former vertically integrated studios found they were vulnerable to take-over. From the end of the 1960s, the American film industry experienced significant changes of ownership that saw Hollywood remade through the twin forces of conglomeration and diversification.

Conglomeration resulted from the acquisition of the former studios by other companies and corporate groups outside the film business. Paramount was acquired in 1966 by Charles Bluhdorn's Gulf and Western, a large conglomerate with interests in manufacturing, agricultural products and financial services. As Gulf and Western increasingly concentrated its business around entertainment and publishing, the company was renamed Paramount Communications, Inc. Subsequently, Paramount Communications was sold in 1994 for $9.75 billion to Viacom, Inc.

The initial sale of Paramount began an era in which the other major studios were bought up by larger conglomerates. Warner Bros. was sold in 1967 to the Canadian television distributor, Seven Arts, but it is indicative of the changing shape of Hollywood at this time that Warner Bros./Seven Arts was sold two years later to a company with no background in entertainment. Kinney National Services had grown out of a family business managing parking lots, car rental, contract cleaning and funeral homes. In a similar move to that of Gulf and Western, Kinney sold off its other businesses to concentrate on entertainment, renaming the company Warner Communications, Inc.

MCA Inc. was sold in 1990 for $6.6 billion to the Japanese electronic manufacturer, Matsushita Electrical Industrial Company (and later in 1995 to the Canadian drinks company Seagram, renaming the organisation Universal Studios, Inc.). In 1982, Coca-Cola acquired Columbia for $752 million, who in 1989 sold the studio to Matsushita's rival in the electronics market, the Sony Corporation. These changes of ownership saw the former studios transferred into the hands of richer conglomerates. MGM however, the richest of the majors in the studio era, fell on hard times. Despite merging with United Artists in 1981, MGM is now the least profitable of the former majors, its position weakened by not having the larger conglomerate backing that supports the other leading Hollywood companies.

With the wave of conglomeration came the trend towards diversification. The popular adoption of television during the 1950s had seen the Hollywood studios diversify into television production and distribution. Conglomeration combined the Hollywood studios with interests in other sectors of business, including the publishing, media and entertainment industries. When Twentieth Century Fox was sold in 1985, it became part of the publishing, and later television, empire of News Corporation. Sony had bought Columbia the year after purchasing CBS Records. In 1990, Warner Communications was sold to the powerful publisher Time Inc., forming the largest entertainment company in the world.

However, diversification was not only the product of acquisition and merger. Although originating as an important animation studio, the Walt

Disney Company only grew to prominence in the entertainment market-place in the 1950s, after starting its own theatrical distribution arm and diversifying into television production and theme parks. Disney grew not by conglomeration but almost entirely through the launch of its own diversified subsidiaries. A departure from this pattern was the purchase of the ABC Network in 1996 for $19 billion, consolidating Disney's position as the world's second largest media and entertainment company. With interests in broadcasting, film production and distribution, theme parks, tourism, merchandise, theatre stage productions, and Internet content and delivery, Disney is one of the clearest examples of how Hollywood has been changed by the trend towards diversification.

By the end of the 1990s it was increasingly difficult to view the American film industry as separable from a broader entertainment marketplace. Compared to the vertically integrated structure of Hollywood in the studio era of the 1930s and 1940s, the era of conglomeration and diversification is probably best understood by what Thomas Schatz describes as the trend towards 'horizontal integration' (1993: 35).

High Concept, the Event Movie and the Marketability of the Star

Despite changes in ownership, Hollywood continues to be based on the package-unit system of production. In the studio era, films could be sold in blocks, with marketing costs spread across several films. However, in the package-unit system, films are marketed individually, with P&A (prints and advertising) expenditure attached to the single film. Figures indicate the equal emphasis placed in contemporary Hollywood on the making and marketing of films. During the 1990s the Motion Picture Association of America (MPAA), the industry body representing the collective interests of the major producers and distributors in Hollywood, estimated that for the films made by its members, the average production or negative cost (i.e. the cost of producing a feature film's finished negative) grew from $26.8 million in 1990 to $51.5 million in 1999 (see MPAA 1999). Paralleling this rise in production expenditure, marketing or prints and advertising costs grew in proportion from $12 million in 1990 to $24.5 million in 1999.

Compared to an average combined negative and P&A expenditure of $38.8 million in 1990, the average cost of making and marketing features by members of the MPAA had nearly doubled by 1999, reaching $76 million.

During the studio era, producers had looked towards novel ways by which movies could be tied in to the promotion of products in ancillary markets, and the contemporary industry has looked in similar ways to spread the marketability of film properties. In his study of Hollywood film in the 1980s and 1990s, Justin Wyatt (1994) argues that films have increasingly become the focus for various marketing opportunities. Market research is seen to inform not only the development of a successful film but also to explore how the film may promote other merchandise, for example soundtracks, mugs, T-shirts and food stuffs. Central to recognising success in all these fields is the premise, the basic marketable idea that can be exploited in the sale of the film and all ancillary merchandise. To describe this close integration of cinema with marketability, Wyatt uses the term popularised by the industry in the 1980s – 'high concept' – which he describes as 'a form of narrative which is highly marketable' (p. 12). Wyatt suggests that the idea of high concept entered industry thinking through projects based on a simple premise which could be marketed to maximum effect. *Batman* (1989), for example, represented the trend for high concept production in the 1980s.

In the era of high concept film-making, the premise would be something that could be represented in a straightforward and uncompli-cated manner. Wyatt suggests that one solution to this requirement was to use the image of the star as a means of illustrating the premise. According to this view, the star became the premise, and the premise was the thing that made the film and other products marketable. So in *Top Gun* (1986), the premise of the film could be summarised as 'fighter pilot in love'. That idea was marketed through the boyish good looks of Tom Cruise, whose face appeared prominently on posters for the film and in the video for the song 'Take My Breath Away' by the group Berlin, a chart hit in North America and Europe. Not only did Cruise's image serve to sell the film but financing for the project also attracted money through product placements for the sunglasses manufacturer Rayban. Sales of leather jackets were also rumoured to have benefited from the film's release. Thus Cruise represented not only the film but also performed a role as fashion model.

Since the 1980s, the term high concept seems to have been replaced by the label 'event movie'. While still describing film as a marketing phenomenon, this latter expression usefully draws attention to the work of marketing in making a film more than simply a movie and more of a national and global happening. At the end of the 1990s, films like *Con Air* (1997), *Face/Off* (1997), *G. I. Jane* (1997), *Armageddon* (1998), *Dr Dolittle* (1998), *Austin Powers: The Spy Who Shagged Me* (1999) and *The Matrix* (1999) all provided examples of projects where star image and premise appeared closely intertwined to create a marketing event. With *Titanic* (1997), the poster carrying the image of Leonardo DiCaprio and Kate Winslet in profile, divided by the prow of the great boat, neatly conveyed the film's premise of young romantics, from different sides of the tracks, striving to overcome the obstacles that stand in the way of their love.

In his discussion of the New Hollywood, Schatz (1993) argues that many of the most successful films in the contemporary market have been characterised by a hybrid mixing of generic conventions. Schatz suggests that where the classic Hollywood cinema of the studio era maintained clear generic differences, contemporary Hollywood cinema has produced films which freely combine aspects of several genres. For example, Schatz sees *Star Wars* (1977) as a meeting of science fiction, the western, the war film and the adventure movie. This breadth of generic references can be related to the marketability of high concept or the event movie. By offering a taste of many things, a single film can hope to maximise its audience by offering something for everybody. Compared to the stable, generically defined worlds of classic narrative cinema, Schatz suggests that some examples of contemporary cinema display what he calls 'purposeful incoherence', an intentional combination of pleasures 'which actually "opens" the film to different readings (and readers), allowing for multiple interpretative strategies and thus broadening the potential audience appeal' (23).

Transformed by the effects of conglomeration and diversification, it can be argued that horizontal integration has had a significant impact on the types of narrative created in popular Hollywood cinema. As Schatz notes (34):

> The vertical integration of classical Hollywood, which ensured a closed industrial system and coherent narrative, has given way to the 'horizontal integration' of ... tightly diversified media conglomerates, which favours texts strategically 'open' to multiple readings and multimedia reiteration.

In the entertainment business, horizontal integration has conjured up belief in the power of 'synergy'. A buzzword of modern marketing, synergy describes the opportunity to sell a single property or concept across several markets in ways that provide for the interaction and synchronisation of promotional energies. Mixing ownership of film rights with assets in television production and broadcasting, together with their own consumer product licensing divisions, the horizontally integrated media and entertainment conglomerates are ideally placed to see returns from numerous revenue streams relating to a single property. In the entertainment business, the idea of synergy suggests that the promotion of a film may sell the soundtrack record, which will help sales of toys and other merchandising, and later a television spin off possibly, all of which will enhance the making of a movie into an event.

In the workings of synergy, stars can be used to market a property across different media. Sony Pictures Entertainment (SPE) made effective use of Will Smith around the promotion of *Men in Black* (1997). As a hybrid mixture of comedy, action, science fiction and conspiracy theory narratives, the film entertained a broad spectrum of tastes across both child and adult audiences. Although the film co-starred Tommy Lee Jones, the identity of Smith was principally used to sell the *Men In Black* concept across various media. Originally a rap artist, appearing at the end of the 1980s as the 'Fresh Prince' with DJ Jazzy Jeff, Smith moved on to become a comic television actor with his lead in the series 'The Fresh Prince of Bel

Air' (1990–1996). After signing to Sony Music Entertainment (SME), he built a successful solo singing career with the albums 'Big Willie Style' (Sony Music, 1997) and 'Willenium' (Sony Music, 1999). Prior to SPE's opening of *Men in Black* in the United States during the summer season of 1997, SME released Smith's single of the same name. With a video featuring extracts from the movie, song and film served to mutually promote each other.

For *Men in Black* the image of the suited heroes, masked by sunglasses (a product placement openly referenced in advertisements by Rayban, the manufacturer), appeared across posters and other promotional materials to brand the film with a noirish but highly glossy style. Wyatt (1994) sees the use of a uniform style as central to the marketability of the high concept property. When considering the use of style in the selling of the *Men in Black* concept, Smith's racial identity cannot be seen as an accidental factor, for it is possible to see Smith's colour, plus his background in rap, as making 'blackness' a factor in marketing the film as 'hip'. The look of the film was therefore intimately linked with its star.

Synergy may be a provocative idea but it is possible to over-estimate its actual effect and impact on contemporary Hollywood and the star system. Will Smith, a mixture of equally successful music star and film star, is uncharacteristic of modern stardom. If anything, the crossing over of music and film careers is more representative of a previous era of stars such as Bing Crosby, Doris Day, Frank Sinatra and Elvis Presley. Smith's example also shows that synergy does not always work. After the success of *Men in Black*, Sony attempted to repeat the formula with *Wild Wild West* (1999). Again a hybrid mixture of genres, with Smith in the lead role and supported by a soundtrack single from him, neither film nor record matched the performance of the previous phenomenon. At the theatrical box office, *Wild Wild West* grossed $114 million in North America, and $104 million internationally, compared to *Men in Black*'s $250 million domestic takings and $313 million overseas.

With further consideration, evidence of synergy working appears confined to examples of children's cinema. Disney in particular has proved adept at marketing the studio's animated family features across many media and consumer products, a success that does not involve the participation of live action stars. Apart from soundtrack singles and albums, adult audiences do not seem to be swayed to make purchases of franchised movie tie-ins. Beliefs in synergy may evoke images of a monolithic, fully integrated entertainment marketplace, with the images of stars used to crystallise popular concepts in the horizontally integrated Hollywood. In practice, however, the actual effects of synergy in Hollywood are quite limited, and the images of stars, although valuable, fail to fully stabilise the demand for films and other related goods.

Case Study: Sony, Schwarzenegger and The Last Action Hero

The Last Action Hero (1993) occupies an infamous place in recent Hollywood history. On paper, the project appeared a certain hit, employing Arnold Schwarzenegger, one the most popular stars of the period, in a role tailor-made to foreground his star image. The project was developed through Columbia Pictures, the feature film production division of the Sony Corporation. Since buying into the film industry four years previously, Sony had struggled to secure major box office success. Development, production and marketing costs on *The Last Action Hero* were allowed to spiral as Columbia confidently predicted the project would give Sony a hit to equal any produced by the competing media conglomerates. When, in 1993, the film spectacularly failed at the summer box office, *The Last Action Hero* raised many questions about the power and value of the star in the era of conglomeration.

Sony's purchase of Columbia Pictures in 1989 was motivated by a desire to secure 'software' to feed developments in the company's main business segment, electronics manufacturing. In 1974, the company announced the launch of the first video cassette recorder (VCR) for the domestic market. Using the Beta format, the Betamax system saw Sony lead the way in home video entertainment. Two years later, however, JVC, a subsidiary of the Japanese electronics manufacturer Matsushita, launched a rival video recorder using the incompatible VHS format. JVC had struck several deals with the Hollywood studios to release films on

VHS for rental and retail. This move proved the deciding factor in the VCR wars, for as sales of VHS quickly surpassed Betamax, Sony learned that control of software was essential to driving the introduction of new hardware innovations. The purchase of CBS Records in 1988 and Columbia and TriStar Pictures the following year were therefore direct moves on the part of Sony to acquire the interests that would give the company a share of the global markets for music and filmed entertainment. Electronics remained Sony's main area of business but the company gradually grew as a diversified media conglomerate.

Originally a star of the international bodybuilding circuit, voted Mr Universe five times and Mr Olympic seven times, Arnold Schwarzenegger's film career began as a cast member in the comedy *Hercules Goes Bananas*, later retitled *Hercules in New York* (1969). After the documentary *Pumping Iron* (1976) provided a showcase for his bodybuilding talents, his first star appearance came with the title role in *Conan the Barbarian* (1981). In 1984 Schwarzenegger began to break through as a film star, appearing in the second Conan film, *Conan the Destroyer* (1984), and his most notable performance as the cyborg in *Terminator* (1984). These films established Schwarzenegger's action hero status. Through the second half of the 1980s, Schwarzenegger appeared as the hero in a string of the key action films of the period, including *Red Sonja* (1985), *Commando* (1985), *Raw Deal* (1986), *The Running Man* (1987), *Predator* (1987), *Red Heat* (1988), and *Total Recall* (1990). Although other stars, such as Sylvester Stallone and Bruce Willis, were also well known for their action performances, Schwarzenegger had a more consistent record at the box office.

Alongside Schwarzenegger's action hero roles, the star had also begun to appear in comedies. *Twins* (1988) and *Kindergarten Cop* (1990) both created humour by playing on Schwarzenegger's over-sized body and placing him in situations that were antithetical to the adrenaline-rushed dynamics of action cinema. These comedies worked to soften the star's image. Comedy was also a component of Schwarzenegger's action hero image. He was frequently seen to shrug off danger with flippant one-liners, the effect of which was to make him both the hardest of the 1980s action heroes and also a parody of the phenomenon he so effectively epitomised.

A further change to the Schwarzenegger image came with *Terminator 2: Judgment Day* (1991). Although the film saw Schwarzenegger return to the role that had made him famous, the role was radically transformed. Whereas the first film had the Terminator sent back in time to kill the boy hero, John Connor, in the second film the Terminator returns to protect the child from the more advanced and aggressive cyborg, T1000. As Susan Jeffords (1993) observes, *Terminator 2* reconceptualised Schwarzenegger's role, portraying the Terminator as an all-caring, all-nurturing father, who effectively displaces the traditional role of the mother.

Schwarzenegger's previous film work had built an image combining the physical aggression of the muscular action hero with a strong sense of self parody and clownish comedy. Whereas the heroic and comedic sides of Schwarzenegger's image had come through separate film performances, Columbia developed *The Last Action Hero* as a project attempting to straddle these potentially contradictory images in a single action comedy. Using a complex self-reflexive structure more commonly associated with European art-house cinema, the film openly explored the parodic component of the Schwarzenegger image. Schwarzenegger appeared as Jack Slater, a filmic action hero who magically comes out of the cinema screen to involve a young boy, Danny, in a series of adventures. Schwarzenegger was Slater and Slater was Schwarzenegger. The film involved several reflexive jokes on Schwarzenegger's image, with comparisons to Stallone, and walk-on parts for many other stars, including Sharon Stone, who had appeared opposite Schwarzenegger in *Total Recall*.

Such was Schwarzenegger's belief in the project that for the first time he involved himself as executive producer on one of his films. John McTiernan, who had worked with Schwarzenegger on *Predator*, was hired as director, bringing to the project a solid track record in action cinema with the hits *Die Hard* (1988) and *The Hunt for Red October* (1990). *The Last Action Hero* appeared to be the quintessential high concept film, a hybrid of genres conceptualised around the star's identity. Columbia hoped the action narrative would not only attract Schwarzenegger's traditional male audience but also, with the inclusion of the boy hero, would open out to a family audience.

FIGURE 4 *Arnold Schwarzenegger*

Nancy Griffin and Kim Masters describe the film as an attempt to construct a 'pan-demographic smash – a fantasy-action-adventure-comedy' (1996: 363). They suggest the film represented a further stage in the softening of Schwarzenegger's image. The action hero films of the 1980s had become a cause for concern for public commentators worried about the possible effects of screen violence. An industry report published around the time *The Last Action Hero* was undergoing initial development, showed PG-rated films were more likely to reach $100 million at the box office than films with an R rating. This market trend suggested a more family-friendly image was therefore necessary for both the film and the star.

Since entering the film business, the elusive power of synergy had eluded the various media interests of Sony. From a marketing point of view, the concept was simple and direct: *The Last Action Hero* was not simply a film featuring Schwarzenegger, it was a film about Schwarzenegger. Sony were set to exploit the Schwarzenegger concept across ancillary markets, holding 'synergy meetings' at which representatives of Columbia's advertising, business affairs, legal, production, marketing, publicity and merchandising departments met with executives from the company's games and music divisions.

With a production budget estimated to have reached $87 million, and prints and advertising costs for the US release in the region of $30 million, Sony had staked its reputation on the film. When the film opened in the US over the weekend of Friday 18 June to a box office of only $15.3 million, the company faced a crisis. It is possible to speculate on several reasons why the film failed at the box office. Griffin and Masters regard the choice by Mark Canton, Columbia's Head of Production, to conduct research screenings while the film was only in the rough-cut stage, as a severe miscalculation that sank the film. Rumours rapidly spread across the press, presenting the film with insurmountably bad word of mouth in advance of its release.

A further problem facing the film on release was that seven days before, Steven Spielberg's *Jurassic Park* (1993) had opened in the US to a record $50 million weekend. *Jurassic Park* represented exactly the phenomenon that *The Last Action Hero* hoped for – a film that successfully sold action drama to family audiences. Ironically, *Jurassic Park* was distributed by Universal Pictures, a subsidiary of MCA which, at the time, was owned by Sony's great rival Matsushita. By the end of 1993, *Jurassic Park* topped the year's box office, grossing $339,521,510 in North America, while *The Last Action Hero* limped home with $50,016,394.

Reviewing the film, Vincent Canby remarked in *The New York Times* that the film 'tries to be too many things to too many different kinds of audiences, the result being that it will probably confuse and perhaps even alienate the hard-core action fans' while 'more sophisticated audiences are likely to never see the film's occasionally funny gags at the expense of movies the action fans will never have heard of' (1993: 96). At the centre of the project's failure were the impossible demands made to stretch the appeal of the Schwarzenegger image. In attempting to entertain all audiences, the film and its star arguably satisfied none. Schwarzenegger was paid $15 million for his role, together with participation in earnings from distribution. The case of *The Last Action Hero* raised questions not only for Columbia but across the whole of Hollywood regarding the security and value of employing highly paid stars in event pictures. Rather than the valuable franchise Sony hoped would make the company a profitable front-runner in the film market, the Schwarzenegger image became an unmarketable concept that nearly drove Sony to make an early exit from the film business.

Star Vehicles and Genre

Event movies do not characterise the whole or even the majority of contemporary Hollywood production. High concept films may achieve a hybrid mixing of genres but in many cases films still appear to fall into singly identifiable generic types. If high concept involves the matching of star and premise, then this idea appears to have a long tradition in the development of particular films as promotional 'vehicles' for stars. The star vehicle combines two methods of product differentiation: the personal monopoly of a star's image, and the familiar conventions that establish generic expectations.

Through reference to stars of previous periods in Hollywood history, Richard Dyer (1998: 62) defines the star vehicle in the following terms:

The vehicle might provide a character of the type associated with the star (e.g. Monroe's 'dumb blonde' roles, Garbo's melancholic romantic roles); a situation, setting or generic context associated with the star (e.g. Garbo in relationships with married men, Wayne in Westerns ...); or opportunities for the star to do her/his thing (most obviously in the case of musical stars – e.g. a wistful solo number for Judy Garland, an extended ballet sequence for Gene Kelly – but also, for instance, opportunities to display Monroe's body and wiggle walk [and] scenes of action in Wayne's films).

It is possible to see many contemporary examples of the star vehicle in operation. Meg Ryan frequently appears in roles as the ever-so-slightly-dizzy romantic (for example *Sleepless in Seattle* (1993), *French Kiss* (1995), and *You've Got Mail* (1998)). Michael Douglas's strong jaw has guided him through several situations in which he has played the arrogant male lost in a world of psychological, and usually sexual, danger (for example *Fatal Attraction* (1987), *Basic Instinct* (1992), and *The Game* (1997)). Jim Carrey and Robin Williams are both used in films which include specific moments in the narrative specifically designed to highlight the comic performativity of the stars (for example Carrey's roles in *The Mask* (1994), *Dumb and Dumber* (1994) and *Liar, Liar* (1997), or Williams's performances in *Mrs Doubtfire* (1993) or *The Birdcage* (1996)). *Striptease* (1996) was a film about Demi Moore's body, and *The Witches of Eastwick* (1987), *Wolf* (1994) and *As Good As It Gets* (1997) seem organised almost entirely around Jack Nicholson's devilish grin.

Dyer (1998: 62) sees the star vehicle as providing 'continuities of iconography (e.g. how they are dressed, made-up and coifed, performance mannerisms, the settings with which they are associated and so on), visual style (e.g. how they are lit, photographed, placed within the frame) and structure (e.g. their role in the plot, their function in the film's symbolic pattern)'.

It is the continuities of iconography, style and structure across the body of a star's films which leads Dyer to liken star vehicles to genres. While the star vehicle does work to reproduce a set of conventions and so stimulate audience expectations in the same way as generic categories do, Andrew Britton (1984) points out that genre is a precondition of the star vehicle. Meg Ryan vehicles work within the general terms of the romantic comedy (see Evans 1998). The performativity of Carrey and Williams is foregrounded in the context of the character-based comedy. Generic conventions also limit the possible opportunities for a film to act as a successful vehicle for a star. Critical responses to Ryan's attempt to move outside romantic comedy with the war action drama *Courage Under Fire* (1996) focused on the incongruities of the star in the genre, revealing the difficulties facing a star escaping any genre they become most readily identified with. For her next movie, Ryan would return to more conventional ground, *Addicted to Love* (1997).

Britton suggests that it is a mistake to see genres as closed, discreet categories: genres can be seen to share similar themes and ideological contradictions. It is possible for films in several genres to serve as vehicles for a star, so that some stars can be seen to successfully cross genres. For example, in the Sergio Leone trilogy of Westerns in the mid-1960s – *A Fistful of Dollars* (1964), *For a Few Dollars More* (1966), and *The Good, the Bad and the Ugly* (1966) – as The Man With No Name, Clint Eastwood played an individual who, in a world that has lost clear moral co-ordinates, lives by no formal creed or law other than that of his own making. From the early 1970s, Eastwood's reworking of the western hero fitted with the moral ambivalence of the maverick police detective Harry Callahan character in the earliest films of the Dirty Harry series (*Dirty Harry* (1971), *Magnum Force* (1973), *The Enforcer* (1976) and *Sudden Impact* (1983)). Here Eastwood was seen to confront the same opposition between the individual and the official social order – the conflict of one man's law against The Law – motivating Callahan's fight to rid a corrupt world of crime by any means necessary.

Britton's arguments would suggest that genres have never been closed categories. However, it is possible to see examples of films in the last two decades which work by mixing influences from what may conventionally be thought of as separate genres. In these films, star identities appear to straddle potentially opposing generic impulses. Most noticeable in this context was the arrival of the comic action hero in the 1980s. Eddie Murphy, Bruce Willis and Mel Gibson combined action and comedy through their respective roles in the *Beverly Hills Cop*, *Die Hard* and *Lethal Weapon* series. While immersed in serious circumstances, in which a genuine sense of peril and suspense was created, the characters Alex Foley, John McClean and Martin Riggs each faced danger with a wisecrack. As the *Lethal Weapon* series progressed, the pairing of Gibson with Danny Glover became one of the most enduring comedy partnerships of contemporary cinema. Examples of this kind suggest that genres continue to play an important role in defining star identities, setting limits to the contexts in which a star is used. However, as the parameters of generic categories themselves are never firmly fixed, so the images of stars can be flexibly used to traverse genres and also to combine a mixture of generic influences.

Agencies and Deals

In the era of high concept or event cinema, the value of stars as capital has received new importance. As negative costs rise, stars become even more central to the packaging of a project and securing production financing. As discussed earlier, since the move to the package-unit system of production, the powers of agents to act as key mediators in the industry has achieved new importance. The package-unit system saw the agent begin to work at putting together script properties with directing and performing talent, taking a vital role in the development of projects which was formerly the responsibility of studio heads of production. MCA may have left the agency business in the 1960s but it set an example for the leading agencies in contemporary Hollywood.

   Since it was established at the end of the nineteenth century, The William Morris Agency (WMA) had remained the foremost agency in the American entertainment business. In Hollywood, WMA's position was severely challenged when, in 1975, five WMA agents (Martin Baum, Bill

Haber, Ron Meyer, Michael Ovitz and Rowland Perkins) left to form the rival Creative Artists Agency (CAA). Where WMA had a bureaucratic, staid and gentlemanly reputation, CAA quickly achieved an image of aggressive competitiveness, ruthlessly cutting commission rates below the standard ten per cent to win deals and sign clients. Initially, CAA packaged television programmes, gradually moving on to developing feature film projects. Along with International Creative Management (ICM), WMA and CAA now make up the big three agencies in Hollywood today, representing the majority of stars in contemporary Hollywood. Although smaller than its immediate rivals, CAA currently maintains the most star studded list of clients (see Table 4.1).

During the 1980s, CAA packaged around 150 films. *A Chorus Line* (1985) brought producers Cy Feuer and Ernest H. Martin together with director Richard Attenborough and star Michael Douglas (see Slater 1997). Following a recommendation from producer Stanley Jaffe, in March 1981 Ovitz signed the then unknown Tom Cruise. Ovitz would take an instrumental role in making Cruise a star. *Rain Man* (1988) brought Cruise together with fellow CAA client, Dustin Hoffman, and director Barry Levinson. With its strong client list, CAA came to be seen as taking a

Creative Artists Agency	International Creative Management	William Morris Agency	Others
Pierce Brosnan	Jodie Foster	Clint Eastwood	Jim Carrey – United Talent Agency
Sandra Bullock	Tommy Lee Jones	Arnold Schwarzenegger	Cameron Diaz – Artists Management
Glenn Close	Eddie Murphy	Bruce Willis	Group
Sean Connery	Julia Roberts	Kate Winslet	Leonard DiCaprio – Artists Management
Tom Cruise			Group
Robert De Niro			Richard Gere – Andrea Jaffe Inc.
Michael Douglas			Mel Gibson – Icon Productions
Ralph Fiennes			Jack Nicholson – Bresler, Kelly and
Tom Hanks			Associates
Dustin Hoffman			Brad Pitt – Brillstein-Grey Entertainment
Demi Moore			Winona Ryder – 3 Arts Entertainment Inc.
Al Pacino			Alicia Silverstone – Premiere Artists
Gwyneth Paltrow			Agency
Robert Redford			Robin Williams – Artists Management
Will Smith			Group
Sylvester Stallone			
Meryl Streep			

TABLE 4.1 *Stars by Agency*

Source: compiled from *Screen International* (1997 and 1998) and Internet Movie Database

virtually unshakeable stand in negotiations. For *Bram Stoker's Dracula* (1992), CAA packaged star Winona Ryder and director Francis Ford Coppola with a script by Jim Hart. Columbia Pictures was presented with the package as a non-negotiable entity. When CAA took on the packaging of the adaptation of Michael Crichton's best-selling novel 'Jurassic Park', the project floundered in development for an extended period of time while Ovitz pressured Steven Spielberg to join the agency's client list. The project went into production once Spielberg joined.

CAA's power in packaging projects faced criticisms that the practice unreasonably raised the price of talent. Ovitz has characteristically rejected such criticisms, reflecting that packaging 'is one hundred percent correct ... CAA set the pricing standard. That was our job ... we controlled the prices in the marketplace. My theory was, if you had all that talent under one roof, you could benefit from it' (quoted in Slater 1997: 108). While super agencies like CAA, WMA and ICM can wield power in negotiations through their size and importance, Mark Litwak (1986) suggests they can serve the interests of top stars at the expense of other clients. For this reason, Litwak sees some performers using personal managers in order to receive more individual attention.

Due to their central role in packaging projects, there is a tendency to assume that agencies have all the power in contemporary Hollywood. As Nicolas Kent (1991) points out, however, agencies, their clients, and the studios remain in a situation of mutual dependency. Agencies may be the mediators between talent and the studios but that position requires balancing the interests of all parties. Stars need the agencies to get work but, at the same time, the agencies need to retain a high-profile client list to support their negotiating position in any individual deal. Kent argues that the power of the agencies in relation to stars is limited because, unlike the days when the term contract made stars the property of studios, stars are not bound by contract to agencies. While the role of the Hollywood studios may have become more concentrated on functioning as production financiers, it is the studios which hold the money, and agents are only rich and powerful to the extent that they can place clients in packages that receive that backing.

Agencies function to mediate between the studios, which supply the money, and the stars and other talent who supply their services. In this role, the most powerful agencies have achieved their status and reputation based on the art of making the deal. In the package-unit system, the earnings of stars are no longer constrained by the conditions of the studio term contract. While some stars still sign multi-picture deals with a studio, it is more usual for agencies to negotiate for the use of a star's services on a film-by-film basis. When MCA negotiated James Stewart's contract for *Winchester '73*, the deal made clear the advantages of profit participation. Since that time, the contracts of stars now regularly include 'back-end' deals. Instead of taking a flat fee when a film is made, contractual agreements may see a star choosing to be paid based on a film's performance. In the back-end deal, the star is not fully remunerated at the time of production but only when a film is distributed in all markets. This contingent payment is based on the star participating in a percentage share of profits. It is the industry vernacular to measure the percentage awarded to any individual participating in profits in terms of 'points' (see Cones 1992).

Profit participation deals will vary depending whether payments are made on the basis of gross receipts or net profits. Gross receipts are all monies received by the distributor from the sale of a film in any and all markets. It is common now for a feature film to be sold in many markets. After an initial release in theatres, a film will appear for video rental and retail before showing on television in pay-per-view (PPV), pay subscription and finally 'free' windows. Any film will therefore receive income from several revenue streams during its commercial life. Depending on the terms of a deal, a star may see earnings from multiple media outlets.

Net profit is what remains after gross receipts reach a level at which a film is judged to break even. However, accounting practices in Hollywood are notoriously flexible in how 'net' is defined, with producers and distributors claiming all kinds of expenses to make it appear that some films never turn a profit. Negative costs, distribution fees and expenses, interest charges, any gross participations, and studio overheads are all paid from gross before a film can be said to have any net profit. Compared to net points, gross points are of greater value, and the agents of top stars negotiate for these.

Due to the artful accounting practices of the film industry, the value of net points has come to be discredited. When prize-winning humorist Art Buchwald took Paramount to court in 1990 over the issue of plagiarism regarding the story for the film *Coming to America* (1988), the issue of net points came to the fore. During the case, the film's star Eddie Murphy described net points as 'monkey points', because they were of such little value that only a monkey would accept them (see Daniels, Leedy and Sills 1998). While participation deals can see stars making terrific earnings from the distribution of the films they appear in, the contingencies of such arrangements mean that even if they negotiate for back-end points, many stars will still strike contracts that see they are paid some level of initial fee.

Stars and the Box Office

Since the earliest days of the system, the American film industry has used the names of stars with the intention of stabilising audience demand. Accordingly, stars have demanded high levels of earnings for their services. Speaking in Munich in February 2000, Viacom Chairman Sumner Redstone revealed that Tom Cruise had earned $70 million through a back-end deal for *Mission: Impossible* (1996) (see Hansen 2000). Further details were not made available but it is likely that this level of earnings did not result entirely from Cruise's status as star actor, for he was also involved in the project as joint producer through his company, Cruise-Wagner Productions. With a budget estimated at $75 million, the film took $181 million at the North American box office during 1996 and $271.6 million internationally. It can be presumed that Cruise's cut will have also included earnings from video and television windows. However, after the failure of *The Last Action Hero*, concerns have been expressed across Hollywood over the value of stars at the box office. With stars demanding big fees and participation in the gross, it is open to question just how valuable stars are for the industry.

After the failure during 1999 of star-driven films at the North American box office, including *Fight Club* (1999) featuring Brad Pitt, and *The Story of Us* (1999) with Michelle Pfeiffer and Bruce Willis, Peter Bart, the editor of *Variety*, suggested that audience taste appeared ever more fickle in relation to stars: 'The public seems bent on "discovering" new stars. A [Leonardo] DiCaprio will spring to instant stardom off *Titanic* or a Matt Damon off *Good Will Hunting*' (1999: 4). While Bart believes that stars remain essential to the success of major releases, his choice of DiCaprio actually reveals the instabilities of the star system. DiCaprio's star rating was boosted by *Romeo and Juliet* (1996), and *Titanic* catapulted him to the forefront of the star elite. Although *Titanic* became the most successful film ever at the North American and overseas box offices, the film's success begins to expose the inability of stars to guarantee box office success. Before *Titanic*, DiCaprio had made a string of low-profile films, including *What's Eating Gilbert Grape?* (1993), *The Basketball Diaries* (1995), and *Marvin's Room* (1996). It is debatable, therefore, as to whether he brought a bankable star presence to *Titanic*. Hits on the scale of *Titanic* are extraordinary and it cannot be expected that a star's name alone can secure such an exceptional performance. DiCaprio's following starring roles in *The Man in the Iron Mask* (1998) and *The Beach* (2000) did only moderate business. The example of DiCaprio therefore highlights the incalculability of stars in the economics of the film industry. The effects of the package-unit production on the star system may be that there has been a shortening of the average life-span of star popularity. Instead of stabilising the market and guarding against risk, it could be that in contemporary Hollywood, stars have become an unstable element in the mode of production, inviting more risk rather than protecting against it.

A look at the top films at the North American box office during the 1990s indicates a mixture of titles fronted by star names, together with equally successful films without any star presence (see Table 4.2). Steven Spielberg's *Jurassic Park* and *The Lost World: Jurassic Park* (1997) featured well-known actors but arguably no stars. Disney's popular animated features *The Lion King* (1994), *Pocahontas* (1995) and the two *Toy Story*

		US$
1999	Star Wars: The Phantom Menace	430,443,350
	The Sixth Sense	276,386,495
	Toy Story 2	208,851,257
	Austin Powers: The Spy Who Shagged Me	205,444,716
	The Matrix	171,479,930
1998	Titanic	488,194,015
	Armageddon	201,578,182
	Saving Private Ryan	190,805,259
	There's Something About Mary	174,422,745
	The Waterboy	147,422,745
1997	Men in Black	250,004,561
	The Lost World: Jurassic Park	229,086,679
	Liar Liar	181,410,615
	Air Force One	171,880,017
	Star Wars (reissue)	138,257,865
1996	Independence Day	306,167,040
	Twister	241,708,928
	Mission: Impossible	180,981,856
	The Rock	134,069,511
	Ransom	129,137,746
1995	Batman Forever	184,031,112
	Apollo 13	172,071,312
	Toy Story	146,198,683
	Pocahontas	141,523,195
	Ace Ventura: Pet Detective	104,194,467
1994	The Lion King	300,352,905
	Forrest Gump	298,535,927
	True Lies	146,273,950
	The Santa Clause	137,826,098
	The Flintstones	130,522,921
1993	Jurassic Park	339,521,510
	The Fugitive	179,315,784
	The Firm	158,340,292
	Sleepless in Seattle	126,551,583
	Mrs Doubtfire	122,483,936
1992	Batman Returns	162,831,698
	Lethal Weapon 3	144,731,527
	Sister Act	139,605,150
	Home Alone 2: Lost in New York	145,769,282
	Wayne's World	121,697,323
1991	Terminator 2: Judgment Day	204,297,727
	Robin Hood: Prince of Thieves	165,493,908
	The Silence of the Lambs	130,726,716
	Home Alone	129,461,346
	Dances With Wolves	122,469,565
1990	Ghost	197,954,919
	Pretty Woman	178,406,268
	Teenage Mutant Ninja Turtles	135,265,915
	The Hunt for Red October	120,709,868
	Total Recall	118,572,502

TABLE 4.2 *Top Five Films at the North American Box Office 1990–1999*

Figures represent gross box office ticket sales. 'North America' combines the theatrical box office in the United States and Canada. Totals are based on sales in designated calendar year and do not include receipts from previous or following years. *Source*: compiled from *Variety* films (1995; 1999) may have used the voices of some stars, but it is questionable whether this involvement represented any actual appearance by a star, and certainly the names of stars were not used to sell these films.

Other cases, for example *Wayne's World* (1992) and *Batman Forever* (1995), appear to be films which did not use existing stars but which, in retrospect, can be seen as significant career breaks, promoting certain actors to the A list of star performers.

Stars are therefore certainly not a pre-condition of profitability at the contemporary box office. Equally, box-office success does not immediately make a performer a star. During the 1990s, Jeff Goldblum appeared in some of the largest-grossing films of the decade, including the aforementioned Spielberg pictures and *Independence Day*. While a well-known actor, it is open to question whether Goldblum himself has the box-office appeal to give him the status of a star.

Based on the number of appearances in the top five films at the North American box office during the 1990s, the leading stars of the decade were Jim Carrey, Tom Cruise, Mel Gibson, Tom Hanks, Harrison Ford, Mike Myers, Will Smith and Bruce Willis. Arnold Schwarzenegger dominated the early years of the decade with *Total Recall*, *Terminator 2: Judgment Day* and *True Lies* (1994), but his career never recovered the same heights after *The Last Action Hero* project. Like child stars of previous decades, Macaulay Culkin had short-lived success with *Home Alone* (1990) and *Home Alone 2: Lost in New York* (1992).

During the 1990s, Tom Hanks remained one of the most dependable performers at the North American box office (see Chart 4.1). After the spectacular failure of *The Bonfire of the Vanities* (1990), Hanks really came to prominence with *Sleepless in Seattle* (1993). While box-office popularity frequently appears to disqualify many stars from consideration for industry awards, during the 1990s Hanks combined box-office success with critical reward. For his performance in *Philadelphia* (1993), Hanks won his first Best Actor Academy Award, winning again the following year for his role in *Forrest Gump* (1994). The latter went on to become one of the highest-grossing films in Hollywood history. After making his directorial debut with the low profile *That Thing You Do!* (1996), Hanks

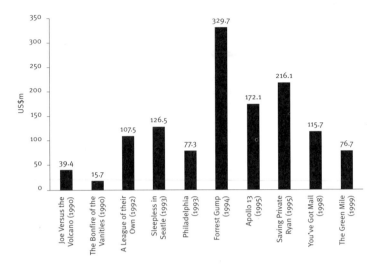

CHART 4.1 *Tom Hanks at the North American Box Office 1990–1999*

Source: Compiled from ShowBIZ Data Inc. and Internet Movie Database figures (1999)

Note: Figures based on the combined gross of the United States and Canadian box office. Chart excludes films in which Hanks either provided voice over work (i.e. *Toy Story* (1995) and *Toy Story 2* (1999)), was uncredited (i.e. *Radio Flyer* (1992), or directed while taking a supporting role (i.e. *That Thing You Do* (1996). Total for *Saving Private Ryan* (1998) combines the initial 1998 box office, together with the 1999 re-release. *The Green Mile* (1999) was released in the last month of 1999 and continued to do good business in the first quarter of 2000.

returned to commercial and critical prominence with *Saving Private Ryan* (1998). Taking only the films in which he starred in during the 1990s, Hanks drew $1,276.7 million at the North American box office, averaging $127.7 million per feature.

Identifying a prominent list of names based on the top films of any year can only be indicative. Working by major successes alone does not indicate if a star performs consistently well at the box office. Bruce Willis appeared in some of the highest-earning films of the 1990s. Willis made more films than most other stars during the decade. Based on films in which he could be judged to have taken the leading role, during the decade Willis's films took $1,258.7 million in North America, an average of $59.9 million a film (see Chart 4.2). However, his record displays many fluctuations. Judging Willis's status on high-earning films like *Armageddon* (1998) and *The Sixth Sense* (1999) masks the many ups and downs

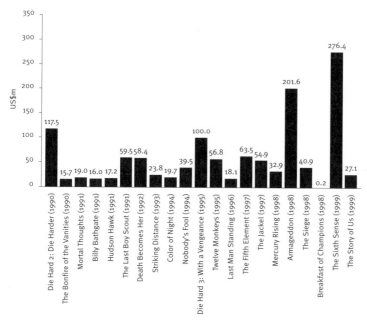

CHART 4.2 *Bruce Willis at the North American Box Office 1990–1999*

Source: Compiled from ShowBIZ Data Inc. and Internet Movie Database figures (1999)

Note: Figures based on the combined gross of the United States and Canadian box office. Chart excludes films in which Willis provided voice over work or narrated (i.e. *Look Who's Talking* (1990), *North* (1994) and *Beavis and Butthead Do America* (1996)), made a cameo appearance (i.e. *The Player* (1992), had equal status with other actors as part of an ensemble (i.e. *Pulp Fiction* (1994) and *Four Rooms* (1995)), or was uncredited (i.e. *Loaded Weapon 1* (1993)).

his career experienced during the decade. During the 1990s Willis appeared capable of signing to some of the most spectacular failures of the decade, including *The Bonfire of the Vanities* and *Hudson Hawk* (1991). Probably more than any other star of the period, Willis represented the economic instabilities of the star system.

There are also many bankable performers who have appeared in hugely successful films but which fall outside the top five. For example, Kevin Costner, Michael Douglas, Jack Nicholson, and John Travolta all made significant hits during the 1990s. By looking at only the very top films of the decade, however, it becomes apparent that few female performers appeared repeatedly at the very forefront of the box office in that period.

FIGURE 5 *Julia Roberts*

Even when taking a broader sample of films, few women stars found continual success during the decade. Sandra Bullock, Jodie Foster and Demi Moore all had hits but Julia Roberts was the only female star to turn in a box-office record to rival that of the A-list male stars (see Chart 4.3). In

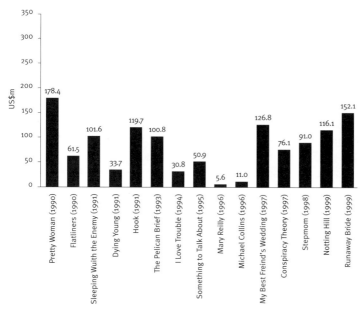

CHART 4.3 *Julia Roberts at the North American Box Office 1990–1999*

Source: Compiled from ShowBIZ Data Inc. and Internet Movie Database figures (1999)

Note: Figures based on the combined gross of the United States and Canadian box office. Chart excludes films in which Roberts had a supporting role or made a cameo appearance (i.e. *The Player* (1992), *Pret-a-Porter* (1994)) and *Everyone Says I Love You* (1996).

the 1990s, films starring Roberts made $1,256.1 million, an average of $83.74 million per film. After her breakthrough hit *Pretty Woman* (1990), Roberts had successes with *Sleeping with the Enemy* (1991) and *The Pelican Brief* (1993). However, with the box-office failure of *Mary Reilly* (1996) and *Everyone Says I Love You* (1996), many commentators believed her career was over. *My Best Friend's Wedding* (1997) marked a return to box-office form and Roberts concluded the decade with the twin hits *Notting Hill* (1999) and *The Runaway Bride* (1999).

Box-office performance has meant that many stars have secured great economic and symbolic power in the film industry. Yet even the most cursory of glances at contemporary popular cinema will reveal that Hollywood stardom remains a system organised by gendered and racial difference. Julia Roberts's performance at the box office stands out amongst rankings dominated by male stars. Will Smith's success in the 1990s was exceptional in a system defined by the overwhelming presence of white stars.

Tracking box-office performance reveals the instabilities of stars as a sign of product differentiation. Looking at the examples of Willis and Roberts, it does not appear that even high-profile stars can stabilise demand in the manner suggested by Klaprat (1985). Box-office performance offers one economic indicator of popularity but can be misleading: stars may choose to take leading or supporting roles in film projects not intended for popular audiences but which offer prestige and increased artistic credibility. Also, box-office gross does not show the net earnings of any film after production and other costs are deducted. If a star enjoys gross points, then the cost of that percentage participation will be one of the costs that will have to be deducted before a film can be judged to show any net profit. It is therefore likely that a high box-office gross obscures how a star's prominence at the box office is bought at the price of high production and marketing costs, together with the star's own participation in a film's earnings. Without access to confidential accounting data, any analysis of this kind is always limited and provisional. Nevertheless, to register a note of caution in the absence of the necessary data, a question remains over whether the Hollywood star system can ensure that popularity equals profitability.

Star Power

From the 1950s, stars were freed from the term contracts that had controlled the work and images in the vertically integrated studio system of the 1930s and 1940s. Power shifted from studio management to the star. Following the shift to the package-unit system of production, stars increased their earning power and became independent producers. Agents also extended their powers to take a more central role in the operations of the industry. In contemporary Hollywood, with great emphasis placed on the marketability of the high concept or event movie, the star provides a key sign in communicating the idea of a film in the public domain. However, the rising and falling fortunes of individual stars at the box office indicates the instabilities of the star system.

Barry King (1986) describes the broad change that occurred in the star system following the breakdown of the vertically integrated studios in terms of the Marxist distinction between real and formal subsumption. Real subsumption involves the direct intervention of capital in the labour process by controlling every detail of production. In the star system, this condition could be found in the studio era with the use of stars as property and the highly regulated use of a star's image. In conditions of formal subsumption, capital does not directly intervene in production but receives the final product of labour. Indications of a shift to this state in the star system would be the trend towards package-unit production, with stars drawn from a freelance labour market employed on single film deals.

While the breakdown of the studio system gave stars new liberties, it is also necessary to recognise that the vertically integrated system had protected stars in various ways. More films were made in the studio era and so there was a large demand for performer labour. As the volume of production declined from the 1950s, then so did the amount of work available for performers, including stars (see Kindem 1982). In these conditions, working freelance could only benefit the stars and only the most popular stars at that. In some cases, stars who did not appear at the top of the box-office rankings – and feared the insecurities of the freelance market – sought to retain multiple-year or multiple-picture deals with the studios. Signed to a term contract, the star would make many films in a year. With stars making so many films, it was possible for a performer's career to survive a number of box-office failures when supported by regular successes as well. This situation contrasts with the package-unit system in which a star's status is only as good as his or her last couple of movies. In such as system, it is possible to see examples of the rapid rise and fall of stars across only a few films. As the budgets for making and marketing films have risen, so stars have demanded higher salaries and a percentage participation in the gross. Stars are therefore potentially valuable for cultivating audience demand but they have also become more costly for producers and distributors.

CONCLUSION: STARS AND HOLLYWOOD HISTORY

Historically, the Hollywood star system emerged out of several developments. As the film business grew in the first decade of the twentieth
century, industrial models of production were adopted to increase the
supply of filmed product. With the industry becoming dominated by the
production of fiction films, elaborations in narrative form revised the
general performance space of film in ways that foregrounded the work of
actors. Following the increase in the volume of narrative product,
opportunities developed for actors to find full-time employment in the
industry and film acting became an area of specialisation in the detailed
division of labour. The industrialisation of film production therefore
provided a general context in which film actors were recognised and
valued as professional performers. From 1907, published commentary
appeared discussing the work of film acting, and from 1909 the industry
pursued the active distribution of various types of knowledge that named
specific individual performers and constructed their on- and off-screen
identities. From these developments the star system emerged as it
become possible for audiences to both *see* and *know* the performers who
appeared on film.

During the 1930s and 1940s, the major Hollywood studios operated as
vertically integrated corporations, using their control of the domestic
exhibition market to force anti-competitive trade practices. In an attempt
to guard against risk, the studios used a stable of stars to market films

and stabilise audience demand. Talent development departments cultivated the supply of new stars and the images of stars were circulated through campaigns orchestrated by publicity departments. To control their stars, the studios hired performers on highly restrictive contracts, the duration of which could last up to seven years. Contracts were written in terms that gave the studio the power to determine a star's career and image. The term contract documented the relationship between the star and the studio. In the contract, conditions would be laid out defining the use of the star's labour and the rights to exploit a star's image. In a bid to resist the powerful control of the studios over their pay and working conditions, screen actors unionised. However, the exceptional individuality of stars could not be easily reconciled with the demands of organised labour. Instead, stars who were dissatisfied with the conditions demanded by their contracts individually resisted the control of studio management over their careers. Despite the power of the studios, it was possible for stars to win some limited victories over the use of their labour and image.

In the post-studio era, stars became an integral component in the design of any film package. From the 1950s, as the volume of film production in Hollywood decreased, it was no longer cost effective to retain stars on contracts lasting several years. A freelance market of star labour emerged, with performers signing deals to supply their services for single film productions. This situation granted extra powers to the role of the agent. As the studios redefined their role, operating as financiers and distributors, stars became central to securing production financing and selling films. From the earliest years of the system, stars had always functioned to differentiate films in the market, but in the package-unit system of production, the star achieved a new importance as the key selling point for the individual film package. For some stars, release from the studio term contract allowed them to grasp the opportunity of becoming independent producers. Television presented a parallel medium that was at first greeted as a competitor to cinema but increasingly became a vital outlet for selling films. Collaborative interaction between the film and television industries established a whole new image market for film stars and extended the range of possibilities through which the images of stars could be exploited and legally contested. The transformations in the American film industry that emerged from this period have continued to define the organisation of the industry today, and it is these changes which have shaped the contemporary Hollywood star system.

Film stardom has never operated in isolation from other sectors of the entertainment business. From the early interchange between cinema and vaudeville, American cinema has always found itself bound into lines of interaction with other entertainment media. Faced with declining audiences after the Second World War, Hollywood swiftly moved into television production and distribution. With sales of feature films to the broadcast and video market, television extended the presence of the film star system into the living room.

Television and print media continue to actively circulate the discourses of film stardom, yet the most rapid growth in the dissemination of those discourses has come with the widespread adoption of the Internet. References to film stardom can be found in various contexts on the World Wide Web. It is common practice for major film releases to now be accompanied by on-line promotional sites. While each site appears different, these sites frequently carry a common set of contents, with a home page linking to pages offering trailers, themed competitions, merchandise and sometimes interactive games. Sites often include pages offering information on the film, which takes the form of a plot synopsis together with profiles of stars and/or the director.

Promotional web sites are directly linked to the economics of the film business. However, film stars are also used in other commercial contexts on the Web. After tourist bookings and sales of computer equipment, pornography is among the most active areas of electronic commerce. While the adult entertainment business has developed its own community of porn stars, the images of film stars are also used on the Internet to entice consumers. Celebrity nude sites post images of film stars and stars from other fields, particularly the music business, which are made available by credit card transaction. The sources of these images are various. In some cases, images are drawn from the period a performer appeared in porn before becoming famous. Other images are nude stills drawn from films. Where actual nude images are not available, some sites have invented the category of the fake nude, a digitally manipulated image – usually of the star's face – imposed on a naked body. Images of this type are also used to give the impression of stars apparently caught in various sexual acts.

The presence of stars on the World Wide Web can be seen to create both continuities and breaks with the history of the Hollywood star system. The inclusion of star profiles on promotional sites make available to the public some of the information on films and stars that would previously have been included in the press book. On-line star profiles serve to continue the discourse of the picture personality that emerged in 1909. The picture personality emerged with the naming of film performers, and the quickest way to find the presence of stars on the Internet is to enter a star's name in a search engine. The name of the star becomes a link that traverses sites, creating connections between many and various forms of content. In the same way that the scandal discourse exposed intimate truths about the stars, so celebrity nude sites entice through their promise of revealing the private side of the public figure. The Web has therefore served to further expand the existing discourses of stardom.

If the World Wide Web has done anything to change the star system, it is through decentring the production of star discourses. In the earliest years of the star system, producers and studios controlled the distribution of knowledge about stars. Although since the earliest years of the system, film fans have produced their own homages to stars, most public commentary on stars has continued to be authored in the context of the mass media industries of the press and broadcasting. With the Internet, the authorship of star discourse is opened out to many other sources. Unlike the institutional authorship of newspapers and television, the Internet provides the individual with an instrument for communicating to a potential mass of readers and viewers. Fan sites have blossomed on the Internet. These individually authored sites provide text and images in what become virtual shrines of star adoration. Also, the Internet offers users the opportunity for an interactive construction of star discourse that was not possible with previous channels of mass communication. Although frequently included as part of promotional sites or other commercially driven enterprises, chat rooms and message boards are offered as free zones that provide an interactive forum for the person with even the most casual interest to comment on a star or film. These forms of on-line interactive communication can see writers publishing their most heartfelt love for a star but can also become the focus for some of the most vitriolic attacks on stars. Message boards will see writers assessing the relative merits of the desirability of stars, for example.

With this dispersal of authorship in star discourse comes concern over the uses of the star image. The ease of digital technologies has enabled web authors to appropriate and manipulate the photographic image of stars for unlicensed use. Even so, it would be incorrect to presume that the Internet threatens the star system. Rather, the Internet goes a long way towards continuing and further promoting the appeal of film stars. The discourses of stardom that emerged in the first decades of the twentieth century continue to structure knowledge about stars in the on-line universe. At the same time, however, digital imaging and interactive communications decentre the production of star identities and in so doing challenge the commercial and legal control of star identities on which the system has always depended.

It was suggested in the introduction that recent studies of stardom have tended to be dominated by the reading and analysis of star images. This book has departed from this tradition to look at the place of the star in the changing shape of the Hollywood film industry. It has been the concern of this book to explore the star as a 'phenomenon of production', exploring the links between the star as image, labour and capital. Chapters have examined the general structural trends that have defined particular phases in the organisation of the star system, looking at the conditions in which the system emerged, how the studios controlled the ownership of star images, and the power of the star in contemporary Hollywood. However, the nature of stardom, with its emphasis on individual uniqueness, always demands the need to move from the general to the specific. For this reason, case studies have concentrated on how particular stars have negotiated their status as image, labour and capital.

This book has drawn on existing research to sketch broad phases in the historical transformation of the Hollywood star system. However, there remain many gaps in our knowledge of the system that require further research. These gaps can be seen to exist across both a horizontal axis, concerned with the historical developments and changes in the star system, and a vertical axis examining the various professional roles and working practices that have made up the system at any one moment.

In terms of researching the development of the system, there appear to be several points at which a fuller understanding of historical change is required. Looking at the earliest years of cinema, a fuller understanding is required of the connections existing between the theatre star system or vaudeville and the early film star system. To what extent did stage stars embrace or reject film? What impact did the coming of film have on the labour market for performers in America? How did the film star system link into the existing networks of talent and publicity agencies?

When looking at Hollywood in the 1930s and 1940s, it is very easy to see the structures that existed in that period for developing new stars and the contractual conditions that allowed the studios to exercise such powerful control over the ownership of star images. What does not seem to be clear is how the studios gradually developed an organised infrastructure for nurturing new talent. Over what period did the studios begin to first set up departments dedicated to grooming actors for stardom or co-ordinating star publicity? The studio term contract represented the power of the studio over the star. However, when did the studios first adopt such restrictive conditions to control stars as labour and capital? What conditions were set in star contracts during previous decades?

Where the greatest gaps in research seem to exist at the moment is on the star system in the second half of the twentieth century. There is a lack of historical research on what happened to the Hollywood star system after the breakdown of the vertically integrated studios. The final chapter of this book looks at stardom in Hollywood after the studios, identifying certain trends: package-unit production; a freelance labour market; the power of agents; the growth of star based independent production companies. These trends are very broad ranging, however, characterising the star system from the 1950s and after. In the absence of such research, it is not clear, for example, what differences may have existed in the organisation of the star system between the 1960s and 1970s, and how those periods compare to Hollywood stardom in the 1990s.

When studying the historical transformation of the star system, there is a tendency to adopt a top-down perspective, which consistently identifies the place of stars in film production through accounting for the broad structural changes effecting the industry at any time. Such a perspective inevitably suggests the power of the industry over the star, seeing the star as simply the product of anonymous industrial and market dynamics. However, as the contract battles of James Cagney, Bette Davis and Olivia de Havilland indicate, even at the peak of the studios' power, the star system has been a terrain for dispute. Due to their dual status as labour and capital, stars have been subjected to the conditions of domination experienced by other categories of labour, while at the same time recognising that their value to the industry allows a special margin of individual power and control.

As much as the historical analysis of the star system must be able to identify points of change and transformation between periods, there is also a requirement to grasp how the various components of the system are working during any period. Exploring the vertical axis of Hollywood stardom involves looking at the interaction of a number of professional roles (for example actor, producer, talent agent and publicist) and the responsibilities they perform (for example acting, financing, dealing-making and promotions). A deep understanding of the star system is therefore called for, which can grasp the sense in which any specific star, and the system in general, is the product of collective work.

Developing from Musser's (1986) initial study, there remains the need for a more detailed understanding of the film actor's role in Hollywood's detailed division of labour. How did film acting become an area of specialisation in film production? What skills have been demanded of film actors? To what extent have stars been trained or schooled in those skills? These questions address the performance work of the star. Following Clark's (1995) argument that the star system depends on hierarchical 'labour power differences', there is also the need to identify the ways in which the work of stars is differentiated from that of other actors. The process of differentiation can be seen to begin in development with the construction of character in the script. In what ways have scriptwriters worked to foreground the roles of stars? Further work would then need to employ textual analysis to look at the on-screen performances of stars, seeing how star acting is differentiated through particular uses of the body and voice, and emphasised through the techniques of camera, lighting, sound, and editing work.

De Cordova's (1990) detailed account of the emergence and circulation of knowledge about film performers is vital to identifying how the system grew from the promotion of star images, helping in the understanding of Hollywood's production of popular identities. However, what is missing from de Cordova's account of the system is the links between image and industry. De Cordova's work ultimately limits the emergence of the star system to the effects of image, tracing how the discourses of stardom constructed images of individuality and uniqueness. What is not explored in this study is how the construction of individual identities was central to the creating the personal monopoly of a star's image. Thinking about stars in the context of production requires not only looking at the image as an effect of representation – the signification of a certain range of meanings – but also the image as a source of economic value.

To explore the link between image and industry in the star system is to investigate the mechanisms that have been put in place at various times to make and manage the identities of stars. Davis (1993) has documented some of the working practices used to develop new talent and publicise stars. Gaines (1992) has drawn attention to the contract as a central factor determining the legal control of the right to use a star's image. This work has offered some valuable insights into how the film industry has managed the images of stars during the vertically integrated studio era. As the example of Shirley Temple shows, there is a long tradition of licensing the use of star images in extra-cinematic markets. This trend has continued as Hollywood has merged into a horizontally integrated entertainment business. These many and various uses of star images suggest a range of questions for further research: In the freelance labour market, in what ways are stars now discovered and developed? What actual tasks are performed by agents when managing their star clients? What are the key areas for negotiation in star contracts? How do those contracts differentiate the star from the ordinary actor? What benefits do stars gain from running their own independent production companies? In what ways are star images now used for the purposes of publicity and promotions? How are star images licensed for use in merchandising and how are the revenues distributed? With the popularisation of the Internet, what new uses are star images being put to and what difficulties do those uses present for the control of star identities?

It is frequently the case, and this book is no exception, that studies of stars as a phenomenon of production have tended to focus on the former without adequately attending to the latter. The history of Hollywood stardom demands attention to how the images of stars are located between both a history of control and domination by production or distribution companies, and a history of struggle for personal power and possible interference by stars. It seems important that when addressing the many gaps that currently exist in the understanding of Hollywood stardom, future research will need to be mindful of the tensions in the system. In one respect, those tensions are the product of a fundamental struggle between capital and labour. However, the battles of stars to take control over their careers cannot be seen as an instance of radical class struggle. Situated in the specialised and hierarchical division of labour, the star is distanced from the larger pool of labour employed in film production. In disputes over the control of a star's image, the fundamental issue has always been who should participate in the profits from the representation and use of the star's public identity. The tensions witnessed over the control of star images do not represent stars attempting to challenge or oppose the capitalist logic of the film industry but rather to become something more than just labour by recognising and consolidating their status as capital. Stars are both labour and capital, and studying the star system demands understanding both the industry's power over the star and those actions that demonstrate the power of the star.

FILMOGRAPHY

Addicted to Love (Griffin Dunne, 1997, US)
All About Eve (Joseph L. Mankiewcz, 1950, US)
All This and Heaven Too (Anatole Litvak, 1940, US)
Amateur Gymnast (William K. L. Dickson, 1894, US)
Angels With Dirty Faces (Michael Curtiz, 1938, US)
Anna Christie (Clarence Brown, 1930, US)
Apache (Robert Aldrich, 1954, US)
Armageddon (Michael Bay, 1998, US)
Arsène Lupin (Jack Conway, 1932, US)
As Good As It Gets (James L. Brooks, 1997, US)
As the Earth Turns (Alfred E. Green, 1933, US)
Austin Powers: The Spy Who Shagged Me (Jay Roach, 1999, US)
Babes in Arms (Busby Berkeley, 1939, US)
Babes on Broadway (Busby Berkeley, 1941, US)
Barbershop, The (William K. L. Dickson, 1894, US)
Basic Instinct (Paul Verhoeven, 1992, US)
Basketball Diaries, The (Scott Kalvert, 1995, US)
Batman (Tim Burton, 1989, US)
Batman Forever (Joel Schumacher, 1995, US)
Beach, The (Danny Boyle, 2000, US)
Beyond the Forest (King Vidor, 1949, US)
Big House, The (George W. Hill, 1930, US)
Birdcage, The (Mike Nichols, 1996, US)
Blacksmith Scene (William K. L. Dickson, 1893, US)
Blessed Event (Roy Del Ruth, 1932, US)
Blonde Crazy (Roy Del Ruth, 1931, US)
Bonfire of the Vanities, The (Brian De Palma, 1990, US)
Bordertown (Archie Mayo, 1935, US)

Bram Stoker's Dracula (Francis Ford Coppola, 1992, US)
Cabin in the Cotton (Michael Curtiz, 1932, US)
Carolina (Henry King, 1934, US)
Champ, The (King Vidor, 1931, US),
Chorus Line, A (Richard Attenborough, 1985, US)
Coming to America (John Landis, 1988, US)
Commando (Mark L. Lester, 1985, US)
Con Air (Simon West, 1997, US)
Conan the Barbarian (John Milius, 1981, US)
Conan the Destroyer (John Fleischer, 1984, US)
Corn is Green, The (Irving Rapper, 1945, US)
Courage Under Fire (Edward Zwick, 1996, US)
Dangerous (Alfred E. Green, 1935, US)
Dark Victory (Edmund Goulding, 1939, US)
Démolition d'un Mur (*Falling Wall*) (Lumière brothers, 1985, Fr.)
Devil Dogs of the Air (Lloyd Bacon, 1935, US)
Die Hard (John McTiernan, 1988, US)
Dinner at Eight (George Cukor, 1933, US)
Dirty Harry (Don Seigel, 1971, US)
Dr Dolittle (Betty Thomas, 1998, US)
Dumb and Dumber (Peter Farrelly, 1994, US)
Enforcer, The (James Fargo, 1976, US)
Everyone Says I Love You (Woody Allen, 1996, US)
Ex-Lady (Robert Florey, 1933, US)
Face/Off (John Woo, 1997, US)
Family Affair, A (George B. Seitz, 1937, US)
Fatal Attraction (Adrian Lyne, 1987, US)
Fight Club (David Fincher, 1999, US)
Fistful of Dollars, A (Sergio Leone, 1964, It./Sp./W. Ger.)
Flesh and the Devil (Clarence Brown, 1926, US)
For a Few Dollars More (Sergio Leone, 1966, It./Sp./W. Ger.)
Forrest Gump (Robert Zemeckis, 1994, US)
French Kiss (Lawrence Kasdan, 1995, US)
Front Page, The (Lewis Milestone, 1931, US)
G. I. Jane (Ridley Scott, 1997, US)
Game, The (David Fincher, 1997, US)
Gay Sisters, The (Irving Rapper, 1942, US)
George Washington Slept Here (William Keighley, 1942, US)
Girl Crazy (Norman Taurog and Busby Berkeley, 1943, US)
God's Country and the Woman (William Keighley, 1937, US)
Gone With the Wind (Victor Fleming, 1939, US)
Good, the Bad and the Ugly, The (Sergio Leone, 1966, It.)
Government Girl (Dudley Nichols, 1944, US)

Grand Hotel (Edmund Goulding, 1932, US)

Great Lie, The (Edmund Goulding, 1941, US)

Hard to Handle (Mervyn LeRoy, 1933, US)

Hercules Goes Bananas (aka *Hercules in New York*) (Arthur Allan Seidelman, 1969, US)

Home Alone (Chris Columbus, 1990, US)

Home Alone 2: Lost in New York (Chris Columbus, 1992, US)

Hudson Hawk (Michael Lehmann, 1991, US)

Hunt for Red October, The (John McTiernan, 1990, US)

I Am a Fugitive from a Chain Gang (Mervyn LeRoy, 1932, US)

In This Our Life (John Huston, 1942, US)

Jackie Cooper's Christmas Party (1932, US)

Jurassic Park (Steven Spielberg, 1993, US)

Kentuckian, The (Burt Lancaster, 1955, US)

Kindergarten Cop (Ivan Reitman, 1990, US)

Kiss for Corliss, A (Richard Wallace, 1949, US)

L'Arroseur Arrosé (*The Gardener and the Bad Boy*) (Lumière brothers, 1895, Fr.)

La Sortie des Ouvriers de L'usine Lumière (*Workers Leaving the Lumière Factory*) (Lumière
    Brothers, 1895, Fr.)

Letter, The (William Wyler, 1940, US)

Liar, Liar (Tom Shadyac, 1997, US)

Lion King, The (Roger Alber and Rob Minkoff, 1994, US)

Little Foxes, The (William Wyler, 1941, US)

Little Miss Marker (Alexander Hall, 1934, US)

Little Teacher, The (David W. Griffith, 1909, US)

Lost World: Jurassic Park, The (Steven Spielberg, 1997, US)

Love Finds Andy Hardy (George B. Seitz, 1938, US)

Magnum Force (Ted Post, 1973, US)

Man in the Iron Mask, The (Randall Wallace, 1998, US)

Marvin's Room (Jerry Zaks, 1996, US)

Mary of Scotland (John Ford, 1936, US)

Mary Reilly (Stephen Frears, 1996, US)

Mask, The (Charles Russell, 1994, US)

Matrix, The (Andy and Larry Wachowski, 1999, US)

Men in Black (Barry Sonnenfeld, 1997, US)

Midsummer Night's Dream, A (Max Reinhardt, 1935, US)

Min and Bill (George W. Hill, 1930, US)

Misfits, The (John Huston, 1961, US)

Mission: Impossible (Brian De Palma, 1996, US)

Mrs Doubtfire (Chris Columbus, 1993, US)

My Best Friend's Wedding (P. J. Hogan, 1997, US)

Ninotchka (Ernst Lubitsch, 1939, US)

Notting Hill (Roger Michell, 1999, US)

Now Voyager (Irving Rapper, 1942, US)

Of Human Bondage (John Cromwell, 1934, US)
Oliver Twist (J. Stuart Blackton, US, 1909)
Other Men's Women (William Wellman, 1931, US)
Out All Night (Sam Taylor, 1933, US)
Payment on Demand (Curtis Bernhardt, 1951, US)
Pelican Brief, The (Alan J. Pakula, 1993, US)
Philadelphia (Jonathan Demme, 1993, US)
Pocahontas (Mike Gabriel and Eric Goldberg, 1995, US)
Pollyanna (Paul Powell, 1919, US)
Predator (John McTiernan, 1987, US)
Pretty Woman (Garry Marshall, 1990, US)
Princess O'Rourke (Norman Krasna, 1943, US)
Public Enemy (William Wellman, 1931, US)
Pumping Iron (George Butler, 1976, US)
Rain Man (Barry Levinson, 1988, US)
Rasputin and the Empress (Richard Boleslavski, 1932, US)
Raw Deal (John Irvin, 1986, US)
Record of a Sneeze (William K. L. Dickson, 1894, US)
Red Heat (Walter Hill, 1988, US)
Red Sonja (Richard Fleischer, 1985, US)
Red-Haired Alibi (Christy Cabanne, 1932, US)
Roaring Twenties, The (Raoul Walsh, 1939, US)
Runaway Bride, The (Garry Marshall, 1999, US)
Running Man, The (Paul Michael Glaser, 1987, US)
Runt Page, The (Roy LaVerne, 1932, US)
Saratoga Trunk (Sam Wood, 1945, US)
Saving Private Ryan (Steven Spielberg, 1998, US)
Scarface (Howard Hawks, 1932, US)
Sinners' Holiday (John G. Adolfi, 1930, US)
Sixth Sense, The (M. Night Shyamalan, 1999, US)
Sleeping with the Enemy (Joseph Ruben, 1991, US)
Sleepless in Seattle (Nora Ephron, 1993, US)
Some Like It Hot (Billy Wilder, 1959, US)
Stand up and Cheer (Hamilton McFadden, 1934, US)
Star Wars (George Lucas, 1977, US)
Story of Us, The (Rob Reiner, 1999, US)
Strike Up the Band (Busby Berkeley, 1940, US)
Striptease (Andrew Bergman, 1996, US)
Sudden Impact (Clint Eastwood, 1983, US)
Sweet Smell of Success (Alexander MacKendrick, 1957, US)
Terminator (James Cameron, 1984, US)
Terminator 2: Judgment Day (James Cameron, 1991, US)
That Certain Woman (Edmund Goulding, 1937, US)

That Thing You Do! (Tom Hanks, 1996, US)

Thoroughbreds Don't Cry (Alfred E. Green, 1937, US)

Titanic (James Cameron, 1997, US)

To the Last Man (Henry Hathaway, 1933, US)

Top Gun (Tony Scott, 1986, US)

Torrent, The (Monta Bell, 1926, US)

Total Recall (Paul Verhoeven, 1990, US)

Toy Story (John Lasseter, 1995, US)

Toy Story 2 (Ash Brannon and John Lasseter, 1999, US)

Trapeze (Carol Reed, 1956, US)

Treasure Island (Victor Fleming, 1934, US).

True Lies (James Cameron, 1994, US)

Tugboat Annie (Mervyn LeRoy, 1933, US)

Twins (Ivan Reitman, 1988, US)

War Babies (Charles Lamont, 1932, US)

Wayne's World (Penelope Spheeris, 1992, US)

Wee Willie Winkie (John Ford, 1937, US)

What's Eating Gilbert Grape? (Lasse Hallström, 1993, US)

What Price Glory? (Raoul Walsh, 1926, US)

White Heat (Raoul Walsh, 1949, US)

Wild Wild West (Barry Sonnenfeld, 1999, US)

William Shakespeare's Romeo + Juliet (Baz Luhrmann, 1996, US)

Winchester '73 (Anthony Mann, 1950, US)

Witches of Eastwick, The (George Miller, 1987, US)

Wolf (Mike Nichols, 1994, US)

Yankee Doodle Dandy (Michael Curtiz, 1942, US)

You've Got Mail (Nora Ephron, 1998, US)

Young Lions, The (Edward Dmytryk, 1958, US)

BIBLIOGRAPHY

Allen, R. (1980) *Vaudeville and Film, 1895–1915: A Study in Media Interaction*. New York: Arno Press.

Anderson, C. (1994) *Hollywood TV: The Studio System in the Fifties*. Austin: University of Texas Press.

Balio, T. (1976) *United Artists: The Company Built by the Stars*. Madison: University of Wisconsin Press.

—— (1985a) 'Part I: A Novelty Spawns Small Businesses, 1894–1908', in Balio, T. (ed.) *The American Film Industry*. Madison: University of Wisconsin Press, 3–25.

—— (1985b) 'Part III: A Mature Oligopoly, 1930–1948', in Balio, T. (ed.) The American Film Industry. Madison: University of Wisconsin Press, 253–84.

—— (1987) *United Artists: The Company That Changed the Film Industry*. Madison: University of Wisconsin Press.

—— (1995) *Grand Design: Hollywood as a Modern Business Enterprise 1930–1939*. Berkeley: University of California Press.

Bart, P. (1999) 'Catch the Falling Stars', in *Variety*, 1 November, 4 and 106.

Basinger, J. (1975) *Shirley Temple*. New York: Pyramid.

Belton, J. (1994) *American Cinema/American Culture*. New York: McGraw-Hill.

Bowser, E. (1994) *The Transformation of Cinema 1907–1915*. Berkeley: University of California Press.

Britton, A. (1984) 'Stars and Genre', in C. Gledhill (ed.) (1991) *Stardom: Industry of Desire*. London: Routledge, 198–206.

Canby, V. (1959) 'How Big Is MCA?', in *Motion Picture Herald*, 21 February, 23 and 26.

—— (1993) 'The Last Action Hero', in (1996) *The New York Times Film Reviews 1993–1994*. New York: Times Books and Garland Publishing, 95–6.

Christie, I. (1994) *The Last Machine: Early Cinema and the Birth of the Modern World*. London: BBC Education.

Clark, D. (1995) *Negotiating Hollywood: The Cultural Politics of Actors' Labour*. Minneapolis: University of Minnesota Press.

Cole, T. and H. Chinoy (eds) (1970) *Actors on Acting: The Theories, Techniques and Practices of the World's Great Actors Told in Their Own Words*. New York: Crown.

Conant, M. (1981) 'The Paramount Decrees Reconsidered', in T. Balio (ed.) (1985) *The American Film Industry*. Madison: University of Wisconsin Press, 537–73.

Cones, J. (1992) *Film Finance and Distribution: A Dictionary of Terms*. Los Angeles: Silman-James.

Cook, D. (1996) *A History of Narrative Film* (3rd edition). New York: W. W. Norton.

Daniels, B., D. Leedy, and S. Sills (1998) *Movie Money: Understanding Hollywood's (Creative) Accounting Practices*. Los Angeles: Silman-James.

Davis, R. (1993) *The Glamour Factory: Inside Hollywood's Big Studio System*. Dallas: Southern Methodist University Press.

De Cordova, R. (1990) *Picture Personalities: The Emergence of the Star System in America*. Urbana: University of Illinois Press.

Dunlap, W. (1752) 'Lewis Hallam's Company and Repertory', in A. Nagler (ed.) (1952) *A Source Book in Theatrical History*. New York: Dover Publications, 509–12.

Eckert, C. (1974) 'Shirley Temple and the House of Rockerfeller', in C. Gledhill (ed.) (1991) *Stardom: Industry of Desire*. London: Routledge, 60–74.

—— (1978) 'The Carole Lombard in Macy's Window', in *Quarterly Review of Film Studies*, 3, 1, 1–21.

Edwards, A. (1988) *Shirley Temple: American Princess*. New York: William Morrow.

Evans, P. (1998) 'Meg Ryan, Megastar', in P. Evans and C. Deleyto (eds) *Terms of Endearment: Hollywood Romantic Comedy of the 1980s and 1990s*. Edinburgh: Edinburgh University Press, 188–208.

Fishgall, G. (1995) *Against Type: The Biography of Burt Lancaster*. New York: Scribner.

Gaines, J. (1992) *Contested Culture: The Image, the Voice and the Law*. London: British Film Institute.

Gomery, D. (1986) *The Hollywood Studio System*. London: Macmillan.

Greene, G. (1937) '''Review of Wee Willie Winkie', in *Night and Day*, October 28, 1937', in Edwards, A. (1988), 363–4.

Griffin, N. and K. Master (1996) *Hit and Run: How John Peters and Peter Guber Took Sony for a Ride in Hollywood*. New York: Touchstone.

Gunning, T. (1986) 'The Cinema of Attractions: Early Film, It's Spectator and the *Avant-Garde*', in Elsaesser, T. (ed.) (1990) *Early Cinema: Space Frame Narrative*. London: British Film Institute, 56–62.

Hagopian, K. (1986) 'Declarations of Independence: A History of Cagney Productions', in *The Velvet Light Trap*, 22, 16–32.

Handel, L. (1950) *Hollywood Looks at Its Audience: A Report on Film Audience Research. Urbana: University of Illinois Press*.

Hansen, E. (2000) '''Impossible" but True: Cruise Got $70 million in Deal', in *The Hollywood Reporter, 8 February, 4 and 113*.

Harris, A. (1994) *Broadway Theatre*. London: Routledge.

Haskell, Molly (1987) *From Reverence to Rape: The Treatment of Women in the Movies*, 2nd edition, Chicago: University of Chicago Press.

Huettig, M. (1944) *Economic Control of the Motion Picture Industry: A Study in Industrial Organization*. Philadelphia: University of Pennsylvania Press.

Jacobs, L. (1968) *The Rise of the American Film: A Critical History*. New York: Teachers College Press.

Jeffords, S. (1993) 'Can Masculinity Be Terminated?', in S. Cohan and I. Rae Hark (eds) *Screening the Male: Exploring Masculinities in Hollywood Cinema*. London: Routledge, 245–62.

Jewell, R. and V. Harbin. (1982) *The RKO Story*. London: Octopus Books.

Kent, N. (1991) *Naked Hollywood: Money and Power in the Movies Today*. New York: St. Martin's Press.

Kindem, G. (1982) 'Hollywood's Movie Star System: An Historical Overview', in G. Kindem (ed.) *The American Movie Industry: The Business of Motion Pictures*. Carbondale: Southern Illinois University Press, 79–93.

King, B. (1986) 'Stardom as an Occupation', in P. Kerr (ed.) *The Hollywood Film Industry. London: Routledge and Kegan Paul,* 154–84.

—— (1987) 'The Star and the Commodity: Notes Towards a Performance Theory of Stardom', in *Cultural Studies*, 1, 2, 145–61.

Klaprat, C. (1985) 'The Star as Market Strategy: Bette Davis in Another Light,' in T. Balio (ed.) (1985) *The American Film Industry*. Madison: University of Wisconsin Press, 351–76.

Litwak, M. (1986) *Reel Power: The Struggle for Influence and Success in the New Hollywood*. Los Angeles: Silman-James.

MacCann, R. Dyer (1962) *Hollywood in Transition*. Boston: Houghton Mifflin.

McArthur, B. (1984) *Actors and American Culture 1880–1920*. Philadelphia: Temple University Press.

McDonald, P. (1995) 'Star Studies', in J. Hollows and M. Jancovich (eds) *Approaches to Popular Film*. Manchester: Manchester University Press, 79–97.

—— (1998) 'Reconceptualising Stardom', in R. Dyer, *Stars* (2nd edition). London: British Film Institute, 175–211.

McDougal, D. (1998) *The Last Mogul: Lew Wasserman, MCA, and the Hidden History of Hollywood*. New York: Crown.

McGilligan, P. (1975) *Cagney: The Actor as Auteur*. London: Tantivy Press.

May, L. (1980) *Screening Out the Past: The Birth of Mass Culture and the Motion Picture Industry*. Chicago: Chicago University Press.

Mordden, E. (1981) *The American Theatre*. New York: Oxford University Press.

Moser, J. (ed.) (1998) *International Motion Picture Almanac 1998* (69th edition). New York: Quigley.

MPAA (1999) 'US Economic Review', On-line. Available at: http://www.mpaa.org/useconomicreview/1999Economic/index.htm.

Musser, C. (1986) 'The Changing Status of the Actor', in J. Leyda and C. Musser (eds) *Before Hollywood: Turn-of-the-Century Film From the American Archives*. New York: American Federation for the Arts, 57–62.

—— (1994) *The Emergence of Cinema: The American Screen to 1907*. Berkeley: University of California Press.

Pearson, R. (1992) *Eloquent Gestures: The Transformation of Performance Style in the Griffith Biograph Films*. Berkeley: University of California Press.

Pickford, M. (1956) *Sunshine and Shadow*. London: William Heinemann.

Powdermaker, H. (1951) *Hollywood, the Dream Factory: An Anthropologist Looks at the Movie-Makers*. London: Secker and Warburg.

Prindle, D. (1988) *The Politics of Glamour: Ideology and Democracy in the Screen Actors Guild*. Madison: University of Wisconsin Press.

Roddick, Nick (1983) *A New Deal in Entertainment: Warner Brothers in the 1930s*. London: British Film Institute.

Ross, M. (1941) *Stars and Strikes: Unionization of Hollywood*. New York: Columbia University Press.

Rosten, L. (1941) *Hollywood: The Movie Colony, the Movie Makers*. New York: Harcourt, Brace and Co.

Schatz, T. (1988) '"A Triumph of Bitchery": Warner Bros., Bette Davis and Jezebel', in *Wideangle*, 10, 1, 16–29.

—— (1993) 'The New Hollywood', in J. Collins, H. Radner and A. Preacher Collins (eds) *Film Theory Goes to the Movies*. New York: Routledge, 8–36.

—— (1998) *The Genius of the System: Hollywood Film-making in the Studio Era*. London: Faber and Faber.

Screen International (1997) 'International Star Chart 1997', 5 September, 1124, 16–17.

—— (1998) 'Star Chart 1998', 4 September, 1174, 22–3.

Sennett, R. (1998) *Hollywood Hoopla: Creating Stars and Selling Movies in the Golden Years of Hollywood*. New York: Billboard Books.

Slater, R. (1997) *Ovitz: The Inside Story of Hollywood's Most Controversial Power Broker*. New York: McGraw-Hill.

Stacey, J. (1994) *Star Gazing: Hollywood Cinema and Female Spectatorship*. London: Routledge.

—— (1983) 'Seeing Stars', *The Velvet Light Trap*. 20, 10–14.

—— (1985a) 'The Eyes Are Really the Focus: Photoplay Acting and Film Form and Style', in *Wideangle*, 6, 4, 14–23.

—— (1985b) 'Part Two: The Hollywood Mode of Production to 1930', in D. Bordwell, J. Staiger, and K. Thompson, *The Classical Hollywood Cinema: Film Style and Mode of Production to 1960*. London: Routledge, 85–153.

—— (1985c) 'Part Five: The Hollywood Mode of Production, 1930–60', in D. Bordwell, J. Staiger, and K. Thompson, *The Classical Hollywood Cinema: Film Style and Mode of Production to 1960*. London: Routledge, 309–37.

Taubman, H. (1967) *The Making of the American Theatre*. London: Longman.

Walker, A. (1970) *Stardom: The Hollywood Phenomenon*. London: Michael Joseph.

Warner Sperling, C and C. Millner, with J. Warner Jr. (1994) *Hollywood Be Thy Name: The Warner Brothers Story*. Rocklin, California: Prima.

Whitman, W. (1846) 'Forrest as Gladiator', in A. Nagler (ed.) (1952) *A Source Book in Theatrical History*. New York: Dover Publications, 545–7.

Wilson, G. (1966) *A History of American Acting*. Bloomington: Indiana University Press.

Wood, W. (1855) 'The Degrading Star System', in A. Nagler (ed.) (1952) *A Source Book in Theatrical History*. New York: Dover Publications, 544–5.

Wyatt, J. (1994) *High Concept: Movies and Marketing in Hollywood*. Austin: University of Texas Press.

Zierold, N. (1965) *The Child Stars*. New York: Coward-McCann.

INDEX OF NAMES

Academy of Motion Picture Arts and Sciences   45
Acres, Birt   21
Actors Equity   45
Allen, Robert   23, 27, 126
Anderson, Gilbert M.   26, 126
Arbuckle, Roscoe   33
Attenborough, Richard   97, 122
Autry, Gene   77–8

Baker, Carroll   78
Balio, Tino   24, 26, 34–8, 43, 50, 126
Bara, Theda   34
Barnum, P. T.   23
Barrymore, Ethel   50
Barrymore, John   50
Barrymore, Lionel   50
Bart, Peter   101, 126
Bartholomew, Freddie   50
Basinger, Jeanine   59–60
Belasco, David   34
Belton, John   72, 126
Bertoldi, Edna   23
Bickford, Charles   78
Biograph   15, 25, 34–5, 129
Booth, Edwin   18
Borgnine, Ernest   78
Bowser, Eileen   25–6, 30, 126
Brando, Marlon   12, 76, 79
Britton, Andrew   95
Brooks, Louise   34
Brosnan, Pierce   97
Brown, Joe E.   66
Buchwald, Art   100
Bullock, Sandra   97, 107
Bushman, Francis X.   33

Cagney, James   65–9, 117, 127–8
Canby, Vincent   79, 80, 93
Canton, Mark   92
Cantor, Eddie   47
Carmencita   23
Caron, Leslie   78
Carrey, Jim   12, 94–5, 97, 103
CBS Records   76, 82, 89
Chaplin, Charlie   37, 45
Clark, Danae   10, 46, 62, 118, 126
Clift, Montgomery   78
Close, Glenn   97
Coca-Cola   82
Colbert, Claudette   56
Coleridge, Samuel   17
Collins, Joan   78
Columbia Pictures   41, 65, 82, 88–93, 98
Connery, Sean   97
Cooke, George Frederick   17–18
Cooper, Jackie   50
Coppola, Francis Ford   98
Costner, Kevin   105
Cotton, Joseph   78
Crawford, Joan   49–50, 57, 78
Creative Artists Agency (CAA)   97–98
Crichton, Michael   98
Crosby, Bing   87
Cruise, Tom   84, 97, 100, 103, 127
Culkin, Macaulay   103
Curtis, Tony   76, 78
Cushman, Charlotte   18

Dandridge, Dorothy   78
Davis, Bette   53–4, 56, 64–5, 117–8, 128
Davis, Ronald   44, 52–3, 118, 128

Day, Doris 87
De Cordova, Richard 29–33, 35, 39, 118, 127
De Havilland, Olivia 65, 117
De Niro, Robert 97
Dean, James 12
Diaz, Cameron 97
DiCaprio, Leonardo 97, 101
Dickson, William 20, 22–3, 25
DJ Jazzy Jeff 86
Douglas, Kirk 76
Douglas, Michael 94, 97, 105
Dressler, Marie 50
Duff, Mary Ann 18
Dunlap, William 16, 127
Durbin, Deanna 50
Dyer, Richard 2, 6, 7, 94–5, 127

Eastwood, Clint 95, 97
Eckert, Charles 56, 58–60, 127
Edison 25, 30–1
Edison, Thomas 15, 20, 22
Essanay 15

Fairbanks, Douglas 32–3, 35, 37, 66
Famous Players 34–5
Federation of Motion Picture Crafts (FMPC) 47
Fiennes, Ralph 97
Fontaine, Joan 78
Ford, Harrison 103
Forrest, Edwin 18–20, 130
Foster, Jodie 97, 107
Fox Film Corporation 40, 58, 60–2
Foy Jr, Eddie 26
Francis, Kay 66

Gable, Clark 49–50, 78–9
Gaines, Jane 13, 53, 63, 77, 118, 127
Garbo, Greta 49–50, 94
Garland, Judy 49, 51, 61, 94
Gere, Richard 97
Gibson, Mel 96–97, 103
Gilbert, John 49
Gish, Lillian 34
Glenroy Brothers 10
Glover, Danny 96
Goetz, William 79
Goldblum, Jeff 103
Gomery, Douglas 41–2, 48–9, 52, 127
Greene, Graham 61, 127
Griffin, Nancy 90, 92, 127
Griffith, D. W. 25, 34, 37, 129
Gulf and Western 81–2
Gunning, Tom 21, 23, 127

Hagopian, Kevin 66, 68, 127
Hallam, William 16–17
Hanks, Tom 97, 103–4
Haskell, Molly 34
Hecht, Harold 76
Heflin, Van 78
Heston, Charlton 78
Hoffman, Dustin 97
Holden, William 78
Howard, Leslie 54–5
Hughes, Howard 64

Independent Motion Picture Corporation (IMP) 15, 34
International Creative Management (ICM) 97–8
Internet 83, 113–15, 119

Jeffords, Susan 90, 128

Kalem 21, 31
Karloff, Boris 78
Kean, Edmund 17–19
Keel, Howard 78
Kent, Nicolas 98, 128
King, Barry 11, 109, 128
Kinney National Services 82
Klaprat, Cathy 11–12, 53–5, 108, 128
Kleine Optical 15

Laemmle, Carl 15–16
Lancaster, Burt 75–6, 123, 127
Laughton, Charles 78
Lawrence, Florence 15–16, 30, 34
Layman, George 23
Leigh, Janet 76
Lemmon, Jack 78–9
Leone, Sergio 95, 122
Lewis, Jerry 76
Litwak, Mark 98, 128
Loew's Inc. 40, 42, 48–9, 52
Loew, Marcus 48–9, 52
Lombard, Carole 56, 127
Lubin 15
Lumière, August and Louis 21–2, 122–3

MacCann, Richard Dyer 75–6, 128
Macready, William Charles 20
March, Frederic 47
Martin, Dean 76, 79
Masters, Kim 92
Matsushita Electrical Industrial Company 82, 88, 132
May, Lary 32
Mayer, Louis B. 47–9

McArthur, Benjamin   23, 26, 128
McTiernan, John   90, 122–4
Menjou, Adolphe   47
MGM (Metro-Goldwyn-Mayer)   40, 44, 47–52, 56, 61, 72, 76, 82
Modern Merchandizing Bureau   57
Monroe, Marilyn   8, 79, 94
Montgomery, Robert   47
Moore, Annabelle   23
Moore, Demi   94, 97, 107
Moore, Owen   35
Motion Picture Association of America (MPAA)   83, 128
Motion Picture Patents Company (MPPC)   15–16, 30
Muni, Paul   54–5, 64, 82, 100
Murphy, Eddie   96–7, 100
Music Corporation of America (MCA)   78–82, 93, 96, 99, 126, 128
Musser, Charles   22–3, 25, 118, 128
Myers, Mike   103

News Corporation   82
Nicholson, Jack   7, 94, 97, 105

O'Brien, Pat   68
Otis, Elita Proctor   30
Ovitz, Michael   97–8, 129

Pacino, Al   97
Paltrow, Gwyneth   97
Paramount Pictures   35, 40–2, 44, 48, 50, 58, 65–6, 72, 80–2, 100, 127
Pathé Frères   15, 31
Paul, Robert W.   21
Pearson, Roberta   28–9, 129
Peck, Gregory   78
Penn, Sean   12
Perkins, Anthony   78
Pickford, Mary   33–9, 45, 79, 129
Pilar-Morin   30
Pitt, Brad   97, 101
Powell, William   66
Presley, Elvis   87
Prindle, David   46–7, 78, 80, 129

Rappe, Virginia   33
Redford, Robert   97
Redstone, Sumner   100
Republic Pictures   77
Ring, Blanche   26
RKO (Radio-Keith-Orpheum)   40, 42, 54, 64–5, 76–7, 128
Roberts, Julia   97, 106–8

Robinson, Edward G.   66
Roddick, Nick   66, 129
Rogers, Roy   77–8
Rooney, Mickey   50, 61
Rosten, Leo   12, 45, 129
Russell, Jane   79
Ryan, Meg   94–5
Ryder, Winona   97

SAG (Screen Actors Guild)   47–8, 77–8, 80
Sandow, Eugene   23
Schatz, Thomas   64–5, 83, 85, 129–30
Schwarzenegger, Arnold   88, 91, 93, 97, 103
Seagram   82
Selig Polyscope   15
Selznick, David O.   61
Seven Arts   82
Shearer, Norma   49–50, 57
Silverstone, Alicia   97
Sinatra, Frank   87
Skladanowksy, Max   21
Slater, Christian   12, 90
Smith, Will   86–7, 97, 103, 108
Sony Corporation   82, 86–9, 92–3, 127
Spielberg, Steven   92, 98, 101, 103, 123–4
Staiger, Janet   8–12, 25, 28, 31, 48–9, 74, 129
Stallone, Sylvester   89–90, 97
Stewart, James   79–80
Streep, Meryl   97

Tearle, Conway   33
Temple, Shirley   57–62, 119, 126–7
Thalberg, Irving   49–50
Toeplitz Productions   64
Travolta, John   105
TriStar Pictures   89
Twentieth Century Fox   40, 44, 48, 52, 61, 65, 69, 72, 76, 82

United Artists (UA)   33, 37–8, 41, 69, 72, 76, 82
Universal Pictures   80, 92

Viacom Inc.   81, 100
Vitagraph   15, 26, 30

Waldman, Bernard   57
Wallis, Hal   75–6
Walt Disney Company   82–3
Warner Bros.   40, 52–8, 64–9, 72, 81, 129
Warner, Jack   64–9, 81, 76, 82, 129
Wasserman, Lew   78–9
Whitman, Walt   18, 129
Wilder, Billy   78, 124
William Morris Agency (WMA)   96–8

Williams, Robin 94–5, 97
Willis, Bruce 89, 96–7, 101–8
Winslet, Kate 85, 97
Wood, William B. 18, 130
Woodward, Joanne 79

Wyatt, Justin 84, 86–7, 130
Wyman, Jane 79

Young, Clara Kimbell 33

Zukor, Adolph 35, 41